THE PHILOSOPHY OF JOSÉ GAOS

VIBS

Volume 48

Robert Ginsberg
Executive Editor

Associate Editors

G. John M. Abbarno — Joseph C. Kunkel
Virginia Black — Ruth M. Lucier
H. G. Callaway — Alan Milchman
Rem B. Edwards — George David Miller
Rob Fisher — Michael H. Mitias
Dane R. Gordon — Samuel M. Natale
Heta Häyry — Peter A. Redpath
Matti Häyry — Alan Rosenberg
Richard T. Hull — Arleen Salles

Daniel Statman

a volume in
**Values in Italian Philosophy
VIP**

THE PHILOSOPHY OF JOSÉ GAOS

Pio Colonnello

Translated from Italian by Peter Cocozzella
Edited by Myra Moss
Introduction by Giovanni Gullace

Amsterdam - Atlanta, GA 1997

ISBN: 90-420-0256-5
©Editions Rodopi B.V., Amsterdam - Atlanta, GA 1997
Printed in The Netherlands

CONTENTS

EDITORIAL FOREWORD

With pleasure I have read Peter Cocozzella's translation of Pio Colonnello's book, *The Philosophy of José Gaos*. It is a fascinating study. Before Colonnello, I knew nothing of Gaos. Colonnello makes Gaos accessible and significant as a master of European traditions of philosophy who then became thoroughly imbued with Latin-American cultural values. Generous quotations from Gaos give the substance and flavor of his writing, and an extensive bibliography will aid scholars in gaining further acquaintance with Gaos.

Colonnello's discussion is comprehensive and detailed. He knows his Gaos backwards and forwards. He leaves no stone unturned in making clear the efforts, the successes, and the difficulties of Gaos's contributions. Colonnello connects the complexity of Gaos's thinking to the main currents of Spanish thought and to European thought in general.

But Colonnello goes beyond his author to raise deep original questions about being, time, language, and meaning. The reader, then, is treated to Colonnello and Gaos as two giants in the interpretation of human thought and human being.

Cocozzella has offered a careful rendering of the text with helpful notes. Giovanni Gullace has added a lively introduction to the work of Gaos and to the book by Colonnello. Myra Moss has supervised the project and added an orientation to it in her Editorial Preface. A useful, enriching, scholarly book!

This book opens Gaos to the English-speaking world. It should be followed by English versions of the principal works of Gaos. This book by a distinguished Italian scholar is a contribution to the special series in Values in Italian Philosophy, founded by Myra Moss.

Robert Ginsberg
Executive Editor
Value Inquiry Book Series

EDITORIAL PREFACE

Pio Colonnello's book is an excellent introduction to the philosophy of José Gaos (1900-1969). In 1938, Gaos, Professor of Philosophy and Rector at the University of Madrid, left Franco's Spain for Mexico, where he continued to teach and write until his death. Whereas those professors who remained in Spain were forced to teach neo-Thomistic philosophy, Gaos and other intellectuals like him, who had fled to Europe or to the Latin American countries, were able to develop their own theories. Indeed, Mexico appeared to Gaos as his *destino*, freely chosen and well-suited for a revival of the tradition of Spanish liberalism.

Among the important theses treated by Gaos, the essential historicity of human nature and a reconsideration of subjectivity from the perspective of philosophical anthropology remain vital in philosophic discourse. The Ariadne's thread for understanding Gaos's sophisticated and original thought is suggested by the original title of Colonnello's book, *Tra fenomenologia e filosofia dell'esistenza: Saggio su José Gaos*[1] (Between Phenomenology and Philosophy of Existence: Essay on José Gaos), for Gaos's treatment of fundamental problems moves between phenomenology and a philosophy of existence. The theme of repetition, that is, repeating Gaos's phenomenological movement of thought, becomes crucial to a deepening understanding of human existence.

Colonnello organizes his material into chapters which, beginning with a biographical sketch, follow the logical process of Gaos's thought from a phenomenology of verbal expression and categories to a theory of categories. He concludes with a critical evaluation of the problem of time as it arises in Gaos's philosophy. Colonnello also provides a useful, detailed bibliography of primary and secondary sources, along with an index of names.

Although Gaos was a prolific writer, publishing more than twenty-seven books before his death, all of his major theoretical concepts including existence, temporality, nothingness, and subjectivity are elaborated in his two major works, *De la filosofía* (1962) and *Del hombre* (1970). In *De la filosofía* Gaos develops a philosophy of philosophy. Its starting point is a phenomenology of verbal expressions, which in turn furnishes the conceptual vehicle required for setting forth the central problems of his theory.

Del hombre proposes a philosophical anthropology which defines the being of humankind. Since human essence consists of reason, philosophical anthropology must develop an account of *ratio* and *logos* which presupposes identity of thought and language. Among the problems that Gaos introduces, the objectivization of verbal expressions is fundamental. For Colonnello, the uniqueness of Gaos's thought lies in his examination of verbal expressions as signs of mental states, volitions, and feelings. In other words, Gaos investigates the relationship between the subjectivity of the subject and the series of psychical phenomena that constitute it. The real importance of emotions and mental activities becomes apparent when Gaos treats of the *mocionalidad* of the subject, that is, of the sphere of will or, more precisely, the kinetic constitution of human activity.

While *De la filosofía* emphasizes verbal expression, *Del hombre* treats non-verbal expression, such as miming. In both books inquiry takes place on three levels: one that investigates fundamental or transcendental categories and departs from the phenomenological given of verbal expression; a second that examines the system of the fundamental categories as they occur in their relationships; and finally, a third that inquires into the fundamental meaning of the system of categories, or of the foundation of the system of meanings.

Philosophy, according to Gaos, begins with "the given," with thought that is translated into a system of verbal expressions. The phenomenology of verbal expression leads to one of reason, which in turn moves to a phenomenology of the cardinal categories—existence, entity, finitude, and infinitude—considered in their possible relationships to one another. These principal concepts are correlates to "the non-," to nothingness and to negation, that is, to the categories of nonexistence and infinite entity.

In order to account for the negative categories, Gaos must introduce a theory of categories. His task requires an investigation of the empirical subject, who explains, poses questions, and questions himself or herself. All this suggests to Gaos the philosophical question *par excellence*: Why is there something rather than nothing? This query, however, cannot be answered from within the framework of Gaos's philosophy.

Gaos's method requires him to move from an examination of classes of verbal expressions to an investigation of classes of objects. Does the objectivity of an object depend on the relation of representation with object represented? Or need we investigate the necessary conditions for the possibility of any and all objects? According to Gaos, "the given" consists of thought directly aware of itself as verbal expression; it is presented thereby as objectified. Objectivity forms the essence of every object. Colonnello maintains that, as a consequence, the problem of objectivity, for Gaos, is the same as that of existence. Existence becomes objectified as the active mode of the being of each existent. "Existence" and "to exist" represent the substantiation of an active mode of speech. The activity of existing requires, moreover, "being present" to a subject. The study of existence and activity leads, then, to an investigation of the constitution of subjects, which in turn consists, at least, in objectifying thoughts. In sum, for their existence, subjects require objects, and objects necessitate subjects.

Colonnello next discusses the problem of time, which he considers central to Gaos's philosophy. Here the author refers to *Dos exclusivas del hombre: La mano y el tiempo* (1945). This work treats of hand and time, the distinctive traits of the human being. Time is the most important trait, since it distinguishes us from all non-temporal beings, as well as from every other kind of finite entity. One of Gaos's tasks is to ascertain the fundamental characteristics of time. Such essential traits cannot be discovered by appealing to any of the scientific descriptions of the passage of time—for example, in terms of extension. Nor is the philosophical notion of time as an *a priori* form of sensibility adequate for understanding its nature. Thus, for Gaos, neither science nor philosophy provides us with a language that suffices for an explanation of time. Consistent with his hermeneutical method, we must resort to an examination of current expressions used in everyday language, such as "to have time," "to save or to lose time," "to pass away time," and "to kill time."

Colonnello concludes his discussion of Gaos's philosophy by asking if there might not be yet another way of illuminating the face of time, as a language tied to the power of symbols, mystical experience, or the illusiveness of metaphysics. If we put aside intellectual arrogance, does the possibility of silence remain? Not a mute or dumb silence, but one that listens to other, non-human expressions in the world—the voices of the rivers, sea, and wind.

My thanks to all those who have worked hard to republish Colonnello's introduction to José Gaos's philosophy in English translation. These persons include Peter Cocozzella, who translated the Italian text into English. The originality of Gaos's thought forced Gaos to develop a new philosophical vocabulary which is difficult to render into a foreign language. In order to make the text more accessible to the reader, quotation marks and italics have been deleted wherever they would not ordinarily appear in an English text. Cocozzella also enhanced the original text by expanding the references and bibliography. Colonnello promptly responded to our questions regarding text and references. His advice and guidance added to the quality and accuracy of the translation. Giovanni Gullace, Professor Emeritus of Romance Languages and Literatures of the State University of New York, Binghamton, graciously provided the excellent introduction to Colonnello's work. Gullace has written many books and essays on European thinkers. He has also translated important works from the Italian into English. Gwen A. Burda transformed the translation into printed camera-ready form and indexed the volume. Robert Ginsberg, Executive Editor of VIBS, strongly encouraged this project and helped to bring it to completion. Equally important, Ginsberg is encouraging the publication of the translation of Gaos's works from the Spanish into English.

I also thank Dr. Sergio Morano of Morano Editore, Naples, Italy, for authorizing the publication of the English translation of *Tra fenomenologia e filosofia dell'esistenza: Saggio su José Gaos*, by Pio Colonnello. Portions of this editorial preface were published as a book review of Pio Colonnello, *Tra fenomenologia e filosofia dell'esistenza: Saggio su José Gaos* in *The Journal of Value Inquiry*, 29 (September 1995), pp. 407-409, and are reprinted by permission of Kluwer Academic Publishers.

Myra Moss
Associate Editor
Value Inquiry Book Series

INTRODUCTION

José Gaos (1900-1969) is virtually unknown in the Anglo-Saxon intellectual world, despite his extensive and significant work as a philosopher. No works by or about him are available in English. This neglect is embarrassing, given numerous channels of communication and the vicinity of the United States to Mexico, where Gaos lived and worked after leaving Spain in 1938 to escape Franco's dictatorship.

Pio Colonnello's book, presented here in English translation from the Italian, may well serve as an introduction to the thought of José Gaos, author of over two dozen philosophical works and of as many translations mostly from German into Spanish: all this in addition to several collective volumes and anthologies that he edited. Colonnello develops his discussion with critical acumen. He provides a substantial outline of the most important aspects of Gaos's mature thought as it appears mainly in his two major works, *De la filosofía* (1962) and *Del hombre* (1970). We hope that Colonnello's remarkable essay will draw the attention of English-speaking readers to this unduly neglected thinker and will arouse enough interest to bring about the translation of his most significant books, which now exist only in Spanish, with a few exceptions in French.

Colonnello's work synthesizes and condenses the most relevant features of Gaos's philosophical thought. Colonnello moves in two directions: (1) establishing the broad network of relationships between the philosopher and the thought of his time; and (2) probing the unfolding of Gaos's thought. The voluntary exile of Gaos is a crucial point of reference, because it offered him the reason and the opportunity to develop his philosophy in an atmosphere of freedom. At the same time he remained faithful to his ideals of liberalism and republicanism which prompted his permanent departure from Spain. Exile allowed Gaos to gain an original vision of the world.

Gaos's intellectual itinerary, in Colonnello's interpretation, is marked by various stages. From his early philosophical experiences to his mature positions, Gaos progressed through Scholasticism, neo-Kantianism, phenomenology, the philosophy of values (Scheler), ratio-vitalism (Ortega y Gasset), existentialism, historicism, and finally a disenchanted agnosticism, which he called "personism."

As the title of Colonnello's book in its original Italian (*Tra fenomenologia e filosofia dell'esistenza*) indicates, Gaos's thought moves between phenomenology and the philosophy of existence, between the description of phenomena and the inquiry about being, existence, nothingness, and their foundation. "Among the themes that intrigued Gaos most," Colonnello states, is "the problem of time and history, or better, the essential historicity of human nature, and subjectivity viewed according to the perspective of philosophical anthropology."

The first chapter of Colonnello's book, "From Intellectual Apprenticeship to Exile," summarizes Gaos's formation and development: his readings, his influences, and the cultural milieu in which he grew up. The growth and evolution of his thought are studied within the framework of the Spanish philosophy of the time, which was under German influence, mainly Kant, Husserl, and Heidegger. But the central themes of Gaos's meditation lie in the area of phenomenology and existentialism. And it is in a phenomenological-existentialistic key that Colonnello studies his author. Although Gaos's point of reference is Heidegger, he reaches unique and original positions that reveal the sophistication and depth of his thought.

Other chapter headings of Colonnello's book offer a clear idea of the themes he treats: "The Phenomenology of Verbal Expression," "The Phenomenology of Categories," "From Phenomenology to the Theory of Categories," "The Theory of Categories," and "The Problem of Time." In a concise discussion, Colonnello explicates Gaos's philosophical position, marking his originality in respect to other thinkers.

Philosophy must begin from a *datum* that is contained in verbal expressions. Any attempt at defining philosophy must consider it "as thought verbally expressed." Gaos's starting point is the phenomenology of verbal expressions. The most original aspect of his phenomenology is not the description of expressions, insofar as they objectivize thoughts and designate objects, but the fact that they signify emotions, sensations, and volitions. Verbal expressions reveal relationships between the subjectivity and the psychic activity that constitute them.

Arguing from the concrete subject, that is, the human being, Gaos develops an original philosophical anthropology, as a philosophy of humanity that attempts to define human essence. Since human essence is fundamentally reason, philosophical anthropology amounts to a philosophy of reason, conceived as identity of thought and language. Verbal expressions, systematically organized, form the foundation of philosophical anthropology. Emotions and feelings also occupy a central position in Gaos's thinking because mental states constitute simple impulses and volitions that give the subject a dynamic character.

From the phenomenology of verbal expressions Colonnello proceeds to the phenomenology of the categories. He examines Gaos's fundamental distinction between subject and object, existence and essence. Gaos views existence as a relative mode of presence, as an active mode of being. Presence and activity are the essential characteristics of existence. Colonnello next discusses the themes of being and nothingness, along with their relationships, especially with respect to the concept of negation. In the past, philosophy's main concern was the problem of being; now, instead, it is the problem of non-being. Is nothingness anterior or posterior to being? This question expresses one of the major issues of the philosophy of existence. However, existence and inexistence are interdependent: each implies the other. The function of negation has always been significant, especially in the post-Hegelian era. Although Gaos holds ideas in common with Hegel, he departs decidedly from Hegel, when he reads him, not in a metaphysical but in a phenomenological key. Gaos understands nothingness as a source of bewilderment and philosophical interrogation but not as abstract non-being. For Gaos, the crucial task is to give reasons for the negative concepts of inexistence and infinitude. His discussion of the foundation of things reveals that such a foundation is to be sought in human emotions and volitions, and not in abstract reason. It is located in the subjectivity of existence instead of the objectivity of being.

Philosophy must give reasons for the existence of the existent. In this respect, Chapter Five is the most important chapter of Colonnello's book. Moving from phenomenology to the theory of the categories, Colonnello tackles the problem of their foundation. Gaos's problem is to give reasons for the cardinal concepts of human reason, especially the negative concepts. What does Gaos mean by *raison d'être* or by "to give reasons for" something? The traditional foundation attributed to the *logos* or to being becomes replaced by a new foundation proposed by existential thought. Gaos ascribes the *raison d'être* of the categories to non-rational sources. *Emocionalidad* and *mocionalidad* form the founding principle of the world and of human life. Gaos adopts an anthropological point of view based on the vital forces of existence and not on reason or metaphysical sources.

Colonnello's inquiry into the theory of the categories takes us to Leibniz's metaphysical question: "Why being rather than nothing?" The inexistent reveals itself as the most important object of existence: it is gnoseologically prior to existence itself. The antinomy between the categories of existence and inexistence reflects the antinomic character of human beings, which is founded on their emotionality. The root of this antinomy is anthropological in nature, and not theological or metaphysical. It does not express the conflict between good and evil on a rational level, but the antithesis between love and hate on a biological level.

The *raison d'être* of the categories is not the immobile and atemporal nature of being. The foundation for the categories lies in the sphere of subjectivity, the non-rational dimension of emotionality. Gaos argued that theory and praxis are based on a non-conceptual source, pre-logical in character—erotic and misological. His argument required a "going beyond" the traditional idea of subjectivity, that is, a reformation of the notion of subject. Colonnello suggests that Gaos completed the process leading to the eclipse of the logical subject (critical-transcendental) and to the emergence of the sphere of affectivity. For Gaos, the notion of an affective subject replaces the concept of a logical subject.

The crisis of subjectivity was a dominant theme during Gaos's time. It was understood in terms of the dissolution of modern subjectivity and of being itself (which was no longer structure, but event, not principle and foundation, but announcement and narration). The itinerary that brings us from the unmasking of the metaphysical subject to the dissolution of being as the foundation of things, and to nihilism, leads finally to the euthanasia of the transcendental subject. The transcendental subject becomes transformed into living historical subject by recovering affectivity and emotionality within it.

For Gaos, subjectivity has a dynamic character. Affectivity is its dominant element. According to Gaos, we must grasp three dimensions of the subject, in their complex intertwining: (1) *emocionalidad* and *mocionalidad,* (2) plurality, and (3) transcendentality. The sphere of *emocionalidad* is the closest to the subject; it is the point from which the other dimensions radiate. *Mocionalidad* is the ensemble of inclinations and volitions in their dynamic interrelationships. The subject is configured as "living activity" where the interaction of thinking, feeling, and willing takes place. The antinomy of the emotional subject generates its historical character. Gaos's historicism, however, does not assume the extreme form of Ortega y Gasset's historicism for which "man has no nature or essence, but has history."

Colonnello has rigorously traced Gaos's intellectual itinerary from the phenomenology of verbal expressions to the problem of time. The problem of time is central in Gaos's thinking, since existence is essentially activity. Colonnello's quick survey of the various conceptions of time in Western thought, from the Greeks to the present, makes it possible for us to trace the path followed by Gaos. Gaos rejects the aprioristic idea of time that orders phenomena and regulates their succession. Gaos views time in two ways: (1) as being in time, that is, being born, living, and dying; this means suffering time passively; and (2) as living time and its relationships with our conscious world. The first mode likens human beings to inanimate beings; the second to immortal beings. Are things in time or is time in things?

Language does not adequately express time. Traditionally, time has been conceived in relation to motion. Now time is grasped only in commonplace expressions, such as "having time," "wasting time," and "passing the time." Colonnello suggests that Gaos followed, in his original way, postmodernist trends. He anchored his categories to an ever-changing subjectivity that rejects all traditional metaphysical or theological values. Human beings create their own contingent values through the vital forces of emotionality that constitute them. Reason no longer judges emotions, but is judged by them.

Giovanni Gullace
State University of New York
Binghamton

A NOTE FROM THE TRANSLATOR

In his book, first published in Italian as *Tra fenomenologia e filosofia dell'esistenza: Saggio su José Gaos* (Naples: Morano Editore, 1990), Pio Colonnello presents an insightful profile of an important thinker of our time: the Spanish philosopher José Gaos (1900-1969), who, toward the end of the disastrous Spanish Civil War (1936-1939), left his homeland to begin a new life in Mexico. Colonnello explicates the wide gamut of ideologies that Gaos assimilated at various stages of his remarkable career. Gradually, Colonnello delves into the distinctiveness of Gaos's thought, as rich in its heterogeneity as it is coherent in complexity.

It is up to the translator to rise to the challenge posed by the interplay of two highly intellectual operations: Colonnello's deep probing and the workings of Gaos's wide-ranging eclecticism. In my attempt to meet that challenge, I have striven, as would any person in my position, for an accurate rendering of Colonnello's Italian text and for the natural flow and readability of the English version. My task has been greatly facilitated by the invaluable assistance I have received from two distinguished colleagues: Professor Myra Moss of Claremont McKenna College and Professor Emeritus Giovanni Gullace of the State University of New York at Binghamton. Moss has given of her time generously, "above and beyond the call of duty," in a painstaking revision of my manuscript. I am especially grateful to her for providing me with the technical terminology. In deference to her advice, I have opted for the term "being," rather than the awkward *ens*, as an equivalent of Colonnello's *ente*, even though I would admit that the Latin participial effectively denotes the individual entity in the very act of being. In most instances, Moss's expert contribution on these nettlesome lexical items obviates the translator's explanation. Only in a few cases have I found it necessary to annotate Colonnello's more problematic neologisms, such as *me-ontologia, entitativo, entitativamente*. I refer the interested reader to the notes I provide for these terms. No less considerable is the debt of gratitude I owe to Gullace, my friend and mentor of many years. It is he who suggested my name as translator to Rodopi in the first place and has been guiding me all along with paternal attentiveness. To say that without him this translation would have not been possible is not a perfunctory cliché. Gullace's introduction is yet another way by which he furthers the purpose of this English version of Colonnello's seminal study.

Abiding by the standards established by the editors, I have expanded Colonnello's original bibliography to include specific data within the individual entries and additional relevant works that are mentioned throughout the book.

While I acknowledge the contribution of others, I am fully aware that the responsibility for any flaws perceivable in my work is entirely my own. It is for me a distinct honor to have been called upon to do my part in introducing Gaos to the English-speaking world. To Pio Colonnello, of course, goes the credit for anticipating, with his timely monograph, the recognition due to Gaos on the international scene. For the service Colonnello has rendered to scholarship, I believe that all of us, his readers, can do no less than to extend to him a wholehearted "Thank you!"

Peter Cocozzella
State University of New York
Binghamton

AUTHOR'S PREFACE

Grief, travail, and painful vicissitudes of existence, such as exile, can create a special moment during intellectual maturation. Sometimes, from the experience of extreme situations, a special vision of the world is born. Trite and commonplace as they may seem, statements of this kind are fully verified in the case of the philosopher José Gaos. From his experience of exile and of grief, Gaos reinforces his intellectual and civic commitment. He develops an original *Weltanschauung*.

Gaos and exile: from this point, I will launch an inquiry that places this thinker in his epoch. I will indicate the woof of connections, of assonances, and of dissonances with predominant philosophic currents. I will also peruse the inner history of a thought that has come to terms with important historical and political events of our time: the Spanish Civil War, the decline of the Spanish Republican "venture," the establishment of the Franco regime, and the flight of a generation of intellectuals toward the countries of Latin America. In Gaos's case, all this reveals why some philosophies are written with quill dipped in blood and upon the flesh of concrete historical life. It is to these philosophies that Gaos's thought belongs.

During the immediate aftermath of the defeat of the Spanish Republic (1931-1939), Gaos was not among those who wandered abroad from Europe to America but never set roots anywhere. He was one of the intellectuals who at first unconditionally supported the Republican cause. Subsequently upon judging that the war was lost, Gaos emigrated from his homeland never to return. For Gaos, exile was transformed from a condition of suffering and hardship to an opportunity for developing his thought in unrestricted liberty. By contrast, the philosophers who remained in Spain suffered under impositions from political and cultural authorities. These authorities allowed the philosophers to study only a select number of subjects, such as neo-Thomism.

Having moved to Mexico, Gaos accepted the new country as a second homeland. There he aspired to relive the tradition of Spanish liberalism. Indeed, he regarded Mexico as his veritable destiny: the country of his destiny, freely chosen and coincident with a plan of life.

Many diverse stages mark out Gaos's intellectual itinerary. From the earliest intellectual formation up until his final theoretical positions, Gaos passed through Jaime Balmes's Scholasticism, neo-Kantianism, phenomenology, the philosophy of values, the ratio-vitalism of Ortega y Gasset, existentialism, historicism, and finally, a disenchanted agnosticism, which he called *personismo*. Even if there is no point in outlining now this complex journey in thought, it is useful to indicate, within the phenomenological and existential ambit, one of the central nuclei of Gaos's entire philosophy. Among his fundamental themes, I will mention existence and the negative categories of reason, negation, and nothingness. We will see how the relationships between existence and nothingness develop in Gaos's reflection. Suffice it to note here that Gaos, in unison with some theses of existentialist thought, underscores how being comes face to face with nothingness. Thus, nothingness becomes, to quote Enzo Paci's observation apropos of the philosophy of existence, "the primordial first, the flowering of light out of the infinity of shadow."

Is Gaos an existentialist? This is a fair question to ask and a hypothesis to be verified. In any case, the reference to light, the flowering of light, does not occur here by mere happenstance. For Heidegger as well, whose thought for over twenty years constituted a constant reference point for Gaos, human *ex-sistenza* signifies "being situated at the disclosure of the light (*Lichtung*) of being."

The human being is the stranger (*das Fremde*) on the road toward the sunset, toward the darkening of the evening blue. "Thanks to the evening," observes Heidegger (who was a reader of Georg Trakl), "the day tends toward a decline, which is not an end, but rather only a direction for preparing that sunset through which the stranger is brought to the beginning of his or her wandering." But the "land of the sunset," toward which the stranger's dark wandering is directed, "is the passage toward the daybreak of the morning concealed in it." When Heidegger is thinking of giving a special name to what has remained unthought in Western tradition, he says *Lichtung*, "clearing," insofar as it is dissolving the concealed. We must not think of that clearing in terms of departing from the metaphysics of light. We should think instead of moving away from the clearing in the forest, from the opening out of the thickest part of the trees in the midst of the wood that encloses it, from the area of light delimited by a context filled with shade, from the play of lights and shadows that expresses the play of the concealment and disclosure of being. Besides, while the Heidegger of *Sein und Zeit* links *Lichtung* to *Licht*, the Heidegger of the *Kehre* (reversals) prefers to separate the two concepts, if only to escape the criticism of a relapse into the metaphysics of light. Karl Jaspers, the other twin star of the philosophy of existence, has long insisted on the method of reclarification as a process of progressive illumination of the dark depths of our existence.

After the high noon of Nietzsche's philosophy, after the image and prophecy of the noon as the eternal instant when the man, Zarathustra, turns his back on the nothingness of the past in order to open himself up to the will of the future, a problem remains. We must confront the *Lichtung* of existential thought, the question of being and nothingness, the flowering of light out of the infinitude of shadow.

Gaos's speculation finds other themes of paramount interest. Among these are the problem of time and history, or better, of the essential historicity of human nature, and the reconsideration of subjectivity within the perspective of philosophical anthropology. For some additional important theoretical questions that Gaos treats extensively, I refer the reader to the discussion that follows.

We must confirm the special perspective that appears in outline when studying Gaos's works. Even without disregarding the relevant influences that come to Gaos from other currents of thought, the vital nucleus of his philosophy is textured with the thematic idioms characteristic of *Existenzphilosophie*. Finally, Gaos takes leave of existentialism and sets foot on other philosophical shores. Accordingly, we must verify the presence of the philosophy of existence in Gaos and the presence of Gaos within the existentialist movement.

May we, and to what extent, speak of Spanish or Iberian-American issues of existentialism? Three general currents of the philosophy of existence have been singled out. Each current develops autonomously. In Luigi Pareyson's scheme, for instance, we find the German, French, and Russian currents, which hark back, respectively, to Søren Kierkegaard, Blaise Pascal, and Feodor Dostoevski. To be sure, other schemes are proposed analogous to Pareyson's. Witness, for example, the genealogical tree of existentialism that Emmanuel Mounier painstakingly draws in its multiform ramifications. Mounier shows a trunk that branches out in two directions: one represents Karl Jasper's line, the other the trend that goes from Martin Heidegger to Jean-Paul Sartre. Of the further ramifications, the French one, grafted upon the old Christian stock of Pascal and François Maine de Biran, stretches from Gabriel Marcel to the poets Charles Péguy and Paul Claudel. Then we have the Russian and Hebrew branches, the first extending from Vladimir Soloviev to Lev Shestov and Nicholas Berdyaev, the second leading to Martin Buber. Among these branches, no trend in Spanish thought claims kinship with the philosophy of existence. Hans-Georg Gadamer has reminded us, in *Heideggers Wege: Studien zum Spatwerk*,[2] of the polysemy of the term "existentialism" in unison with the many theoretical perspectives that come together to form its speculative horizon.

But what, concretely, are the relations between *Existenzphilosophie* and the Spanish thinkers of the Republican exile? If the influence Heidegger and Jaspers have exercised on Spanish-American thought is of interest, I must verify the interaction, which appears in Gaos's reflection, between the problematic nature of phenomenality and the themes of existence, temporality, and subjectivity.

This is not a matter of verifying an historiographical thesis, as if I wanted to indicate the hidden or the last dazzling flashes of a luminous speculative season. I don't aspire to redesign the map of existentialism up to reincorporating fragments and minor islands in its vast and variegated archipelago. What I am really after is the reconsideration of an essentially theoretical question by means of probing particular aspects of contemporary thought. I am concerned about the class of the negative and the double alternative to which thought relates the negative itself, insofar as thought is able to identify either with the ideal fulcrum of progress or with the way of defeat and loss. Above all, the question remains about the negative or negation pure and simple, and about nothingness. What fascinated Gottfried Wilhelm von Leibniz as much as Heidegger and Gaos, and continues to fascinate me as well, is the cardinal question: "Why being rather than nothing?" For my part, I turn the same question back to José Gaos. While on a journey about thought, I travel again through the tracks of an adventure that closely concerns all of us, in our humanness.

One

FROM INTELLECTUAL "APPRENTICESHIP" TO EXILE

In 1938, as a consequence of the defeat his fellow Republicans suffered at the hands of General Francisco Franco's nationalists,[3] José Gaos, at the peak of his career, Professor and Rector at the University of Madrid, emigrated from Spain to Mexico. Similarly, many other Spanish intellectuals, members of the so-called "generation of '27," also known, because of the effects of the Civil War (1936-1939), as the "generation of the Republican exile,"[4] were forced to abandon Spain and take up residence, most of them permanently, in Latin America. Only a few would select the United States as their destination, and still fewer, Europe. If we go by José Ortega y Gasset's historiographical distinction via generations, this is the third generation of Spanish intellectuals since the turn of the century. The tragic events of the Civil War did not spare, however, even the most eminent representatives of the previous generations of 1898 and 1914. Consider, for example, Miguel de Unamuno, a thinker of great originality, valued by many as a harbinger of a literary existentialism, more dramatic than ontological; or Ortega y Gasset himself, who, in 1936, left Spain and resided first in France, then in Holland, Argentina, Portugal, and Germany.[5]

While the philosophers who remained in Spain were enjoined in no uncertain terms by the cultural-political authorities to teach exclusively neo-Thomism in the universities, Gaos, like some other philosophers, fellow expatriates in South America, enjoyed complete freedom to develop his own thought.[6] During the decades of the 1930s and the 1940s in Latin America, the philosophical evolution of the Hispanic-American thinkers followed a common pattern: from Ortega's rational-vitalism, or *racio-historicismo*, as Gaos defines it, to the philosophy of existence. The theses of existentialism and of the "existentialist" Martin Heidegger are a constant, not only for Gaos, but also for Juan David García Bacca, another Spanish thinker, who lived in exile in Quito, in Mexico City, and then, in Caracas.[7] The same may be said of Federico Riu and Juan A. Nuño, the two other philosophers often mentioned within the sphere of Heidegger's influence. I could cite other intellectuals.[8] Of special importance here is to grasp, in the light of the historical-cultural *milieu* of the time, the genesis and causes of the intellectual formation of José Gaos.

Born in 1900, at Gijón (Asturias), Gaos lived until the age of fifteen in the house of maternal relatives, at Oviedo, where he attended the Colegio de Santo Domingo. In October of 1915, he moved to Valencia to live with his parents. This year marks young Gaos's first encounter with philosophy: he read *Curso de filosofía elemental*[9] by the Catalan Jaime Balmes in an edition published by Garnier, the renowned French firm.[10] Balmes's work, which attained great recognition in the nineteenth century, represented a philosophical "summa" in its own right. Balmes endeavored to investigate philosophy's great problems, as arranged into three ideal classes: "criteriology,"[11] "ontology," and "ideology." The young reader could hardly remain indifferent to Balmes's eclectic effort to reconcile and to complete Scholasticism with modern thought, in particular, with René Descartes, Nicolas Malebranche, Gottfried Wilhelm Leibniz, Immanuel Kant, and the exponents of the Scottish philosophy of common sense. It is certain that around 1915, the newest and most important philosophical works were Edmund Husserl's *Ideen zu einer reinen Phänomenologie und phänomeno-logischen Philosophie*,[12] and Max Scheler's *Der Formalismus in der Ethik und die materiale Wertethik*.[13] But in Spain, these works were little circulated or scarcely known.

Gaos's first intellectual formation was fostered by the books that he read in his father's library. Gaos's father was a professional jurist, specializing in mortgage law. He was also an unabashed liberal, who owned many philosophical volumes. These included, besides the universal classics, works by Hippolyte Adolphe Taine, Arthur Schopenhauer, Friedrich Wilhelm Nietzsche, not to mention the volumes of the Spanish *Krausistas* of the 1800s. The leading "Krausists," from Julián Sanz del Río to Francisco Giner de los Ríos, from Emilio Castelar to Francisco de Paula Canalejas and Nicolás Salmerón, broke with traditional Scholasticism, and popularized, throughout the Iberian peninsula, Karl Christian Friedrich Krause's "panentheism,"[14] which carried with it a religious, moral, and social palingenesis.[15] It was not an accident that Krausism found a fertile, cultural terrain in the Spain of the second half of the nineteenth century, which was racked by political turmoil. Krausism was configured, indeed, as the fountainhead of the liberalism that thrived in Spain during that period, and it gave life to the concrete social and political renewal which, in 1873, led to the birth of the Republic. Among the Krausists of the twentieth century, we should remember Manuel García Morente, who would exercise a profound influence on the young Gaos. Even before he moved to Madrid, where he continued his studies of philosophy, Gaos, nourished by his readings in Valencia, became convinced that the German neo-Kantians had the last word in philosophy. Especially conducive to Gaos's conviction were Wilhelm Windelband's *Lehrbuch der Geschichte der Philosophie*[16] and García Morente's two monographs: *La filosofía de Kant* and *La filosofía de Henri Bergson*. Gaos himself recalls how "keeping abreast of the times" ("estar al día"), or "being au courant," became the byword of the Spanish intelligentsia of the first decades of the century.

In 1921, at the outset of the academic year in Madrid, Gaos's meeting with García Morente proved decisive. Morente devoted one day a week to explain Husserl's phenomenology. But, just as soon as Gaos was introduced to the study of Husserl, he realized that a purely Husserlian phenomenology was not considered the lodestar of Spanish cultural life. That distinction was bestowed, on the contrary, upon Scheler's realistic version of phenomenology, corroborated by Nicolai Hartmann's special version of the neo-Kantian theory of knowledge. The result was an integration of Scheler's and Hartmann's philosophies of value. For about ten years thence, Gaos lived a synthesis of realist phenomenology as the philosophical truth. This period corresponded to his translation of Aloys Müller's *Einleitung in die Philosophie*[17] into Spanish.[18] Educated in the school of Scheler and Hartmann, Müller was the ideal exponent of their philosophies of value.

In 1923, Gaos received a licentiate in philosophy from the University of Madrid. In 1928, after a year's lectureship on the Faculté de Lettres at the University of Montpellier, France, he earned a doctorate in philosophy from the University of Madrid. For his dissertation, he wrote a critique of Husserl's "psychologism."[19] This is the only book that Gaos published in Spain.[20] That same year he became a tenured professor of philosophy in the Instituto de Enseñanza Media in León. In 1930, Gaos was appointed professor at the University of Zaragoza, and in 1933, he obtained tenure, with the same rank, at the University of Madrid. From 1936 to 1938, he was also rector of this institution. About 1930, Gaos began to learn Martin Heidegger's thought, and between 1933 and 1935, the ideas of Wilhelm Dilthey. In sum, Gaos successively lived, as "the Truth," Balmes's Scholasticism, neo-Kantianism, the phenomenology and philosophy of values, as well as, with some reservations, existentialism and historicism. In his *Confesiones profesionales*, Gaos underscores having lived Scholasticism, neo-Kantianism, and so forth, as truth in flesh and blood, because time and again, that truth was embodied in the life of his teachers, who belonged to different generations.[21]

José Ortega y Gasset, Manuel García Morente, and Xavier Zubiri y Apalátegui stand out among Gaos's teachers. Without going into an exposition of their thought, it would be appropriate to touch upon the special interests which they exhibited during the decades of the 1920s and the 1930s. Zubiri, born in 1898, was a contemporary of Gaos. But after having completed studies in Rome, Italy, Belgium, France, and Germany, Zubiri was already a highly regarded scholar of phenomenology. His first work, the unpublished thesis for the licentiate in philosophy, which he received at Louvain in 1921, considered the problem of objectivity after Husserl, from the logical point of view.[22] Zubiri's doctoral dissertation, developed at Madrid in 1921 under the direction of Ortega y Gasset, and published two years later, was intended to be an essay on a phenomenological theory of judgment.[23] The formation of Zubiri's phenomenology was also enriched by his cultural concerns and multifarious interests. He studied classical philosophy, under the guidance of Werner Jaeger, and evaluated neo-Scholasticism. Empowered from the lesson he had learned from Husserl, the Zubiri of those years took an unequivocal polemic stance against scientism and psychologism. No less polemical was his attitude toward the idealism of modern philosophy, which, in his opinion, would have led to subjectivism. It is another story whether, for this Spanish thinker, the antidote for scientism and subjective idealism was Scholastic or neo-Scholastic realism. Perhaps, on the contrary, an integral realism, which understands the human being as a thinking and acting, willing and feeling subject, was the solution to subjectivism; or possibly, in the words of Alfonso López Quintás, "a structural-genetic realism, in which the dialectic of reality or knowledge is prominent."[24]

Between 1921 and 1923, Zubiri regarded Husserl's as the quintessential philosophy. This helps explain why Gaos found perfectly suitable the dissertation topic, the critique of Husserl's psychologism, which García Morente and Zubiri had proposed to him, with the blessing of Ortega y Gasset. Not by chance after 1923, was Gaos's philosophical horizon constituted for about ten years by the phenomenological thought of Husserl, Franz Brentano, Bernhard Bolzano, and other scholars, such as Scheler, in direct line from the common phenomenological root. The components of this formation would continue to make their presence felt, uninterruptedly, until as late as the last courses that Gaos taught in Mexico. In these, he proceeded from the phenomenology of verbal expressions to the classes of the objects, given by the classes of the verbal expressions themselves.

Toward Ortega y Gasset, Gaos time and again exhibited the behavior of a disciple toward his master. Ortega's vast production, consisting, in the main, of numerous philosophical essays, is well known. I see no need to review it here at length, lest I exceed the limits of the present monograph.[25] I note, instead, how at that time Ortega was evolving in a manner all his own. He communicated important themes, which enlivened the European philosophy of the epoch, to the young generations of Spanish intellectuals. I am referring to Ortega's special interest in the dialectical relation between life and forms, and to the theme of "perspectivism" that already had constituted the problematic horizon of issues, presented by Nietzsche, late in his career. Did Ortega intend to substitute for the primacy of substance, the primacy of perspective? "When will they ever be persuaded," he writes, "that the world's definitive being is neither matter nor spirit, nor any determinate thing, but instead a perspective? God is the perspective and the hierarchy: Satan's sin was an error of perspective."[26] Vital reason is a focal point of the perspectives that are created in different situations.[27] For the central nucleus of his idea of perspectivism and subjectivism in philosophy, Gaos would declare himself debtor more to the reading of Ortega's prologue to his *Meditaciones del Quijote* than to Nietzsche's works, which Gaos read in Spanish translation.

I would be hard put to include Ortega in the company of the artist-philosophers, or amid the so-called post-Nietzschean philosophers of life. Finding consonances between the Spanish thinker and Wilhelm Dilthey is much easier. These agreements occur when, for Ortega, reason is not the pure Kantian reason that has been subjected to a complete reform: vital reason is historical and systematic. Insofar as the wellspring of vital projects developed dialectically in relation to the circumstance, the subject itself is poles apart from the pure self.

Dilthey's influence upon the school of Madrid[28] will appear all the more important when we underscore the presence of Dilthey's themes in the thought of the mature Gaos.

Ortega is among the early Spanish thinkers that at first felt the fascination for neo-Kantianism, phenomenology, and existentialism but quickly afterwards assumed a critical distance from these directions of thought. They mark the stages in the intellectual formation of Gaos and of other young philosophers of the Madrid school.

The first decisive encounter between Ortega and Gaos occurred during the academic year of 1923-1924, when the young pupil took Ortega's course in metaphysics. Ortega alternated themes on love with commentary on Henri Bergson's *Essai*.[29] Without doubt, the selection of these materials was determined by interests of Ortega. At that time, he was absorbed in the study of love and of Don Juan.[30] In the *Confesiones*, Gaos, while recalling those years of intellectual apprenticeship, considers that Ortega then felt Scheler's influence in the direction of a metaphysics of love. To put it more precisely, Gaos was thinking about a metaphysics founded on the cognitive power of the intentional life of love.

The relations between Gaos and Ortega were consolidated, meanwhile, from a biographical point of view: the young Gaos became editor of the *Revista de Occidente*, founded by Ortega in 1923. Despite this linkage, a first alienation was to emerge from the diverse positions assumed by the two philosopher-friends regarding the Spanish political events of the time.

Gaos's first true teacher in philosophy was Manuel García Morente, a teacher *par excellence*.[31] We must delineate a panorama, even if rapid and incomplete, of García Morente's philosophical interests. This picture helps illuminate the cultural climate in which the formation of Gaos took place. At Marburg, the young García Morente was a student of Hermann Cohen, Paul Natorp, and Ernst Cassirer. Morente doubtless felt the influence of Kantianism and neo-Kantianism, as demonstrated by his doctoral dissertation on Kant's aesthetics (1912)[32] and by his book *La filosofía de Kant: Una introducción a la filosofía* (1917).[33] From the early 1920s until the inception of the Spanish Civil War, Morente, who had also studied in Paris, under the guidance of Émile Boutroux, Lucien Lévy-Bruhl, and Henri Bergson, reelaborated in an original way, beyond the Bergsonian lens, the fundamental themes of phenomenology. García Morente was attracted by Scheler's thought and by Husserl's attempt to construct an ontology of life. Eventually, however, he led the phenomenological perspective back to an existential horizon that oscillated between Heideggerian thought and Ortega's rational-vitalism.

According to García Morente, two diverse methodological approaches to the root of the problem of ontology are possible: (1) a Scholastic method, that is, the dialectical analysis of the very notion of being; and (2) consistent with Heideggerian theses, a reflection that originates from our life, from our reality as beings, living in relationship to other beings. Life becomes the starting point of ontology. We can find many consonances between the thought of García Morente and of Heidegger. From Heidegger, the Spanish philosopher accepts the "ontic" and ontological characterization of existence—"la existencia, pues, en su totalidad, comprende lo óntico, porque me comprende a mí también,"[34] (existence, then, in its totality, comprises the ontic because it comprises me, also) —as the idea that the fundamental ontological structure of life is primordial temporality:

> We have come to the most important point: life's ontological structure has as its fundamental element, as its root, something which is exactly the opposite, the polar opposite to the type of static and immobile being of Parmenides. At its root level, life comprises time. Existence, the being of human existence, speaking in Heideggerian terms, or, what is equivalent: life's ontological structure is time. . . . Time is a word that signifies many things. We must distinguish two classes of time: the time there is in life and the time that life is.[35]

Morente also maintains, in agreement with Heidegger, that the contradictions inherent in the primordial ontological entity, which is life, culminate in contradiction by antonomasia, between being and nothing: "esas structuras [*sic*] contradictorias culminan en la contradicción entre el ser y la nada." Accordingly, Morente repeats, as does the author of *Was ist Metaphysik?*,[36] the fundamental metaphysical question: Why being and not nothing? Without overestimating these consonances, even disregarding them, it would be valuable to clarify an original existential metaphysics in García Morente's mature work. But this task exceeds the limits of my theme.

As Gaos's teacher, García Morente succeeded in arousing in his young pupil a live interest for philosophy, especially for phenomenological thought. García Morente constantly encouraged Gaos to prepare written essays, which Morente criticized in class. One of these assignments became the first brief article written by Gaos, in 1921, under the title, "Análisis psicólogico del acto voluntario," which proposed "to go to things themselves." With its obvious limitations, the "análisis" shows an orientation more toward phenomenological than psychological method. The conception of existence as active mode, barely adumbrated at this stage, and the idea of the presence of the subject to itself as volitional activity will constitute leading themes in Gaos's speculation.

At the urging of his teachers and, above all, of Zubiri, Gaos turned his attention to the classics of Greek philosophy. Zubiri encouraged his young colleague, already a professor at the University of Zaragoza, to study Aristotle. While Gaos pursued his studies and even during the first years of Zubiri's teaching, almost no one among the faculty of Madrid showed interest in Aristotelian thought. The diffusion of Franz Brentano's thought, the publication of Werner Jaeger's *Aristoteles*,[37] and especially the thought of Heidegger stood out as timely, if not necessary, to the revival of Aristotelianism in Spain. The Spanish universities did not harbor any great interest in medieval and Scholastic philosophy. Still, individuals, like Gaos, held that Scholasticism had a clear technical superiority over modern philosophy. They thought that, technically speaking, the only modern philosophers that could compete with the medieval thinkers were the "Scholastics," such as Georg Wilhelm Friedrich Hegel. Probably, these ideas, more than autonomous theses, were a carry-over of the influence of Husserl's and Heidegger's theses.

However, the study of modern philosophy and its history was not neglected in *fin-de-siècle* Spain. Gaos acknowledges his special debt to René Descartes. From the *Discours de la méthode*,[38] Gaos borrowed the idea of the relations between philosophy and autobiography or confession. To Kant, Gaos owes the anthropological conception of philosophy, the intuition of the relations between pure reason and practical reason, and the idea of the antinomies. Gaos devises for himself, quite appropriately, the name of "re-Kantian," not to be confused with any strict neo-Kantianism.[39] Hegel occupies, then, a place of highest prominence, insofar as the thought that thinks contradiction is crucial for Gaos.

Gaos's interests turned also to modern and contemporary English philosophy, as much neglected by the faculty at Madrid as were Aristotle and the Scholastics. Thus Gaos initiated in his course, Introduction to Philosophy, a timid reaction against this neglect, with explication and comment on the *Dialogues between Hylas and Philonous*[40] by George Berkeley.

No doubt, beyond Husserl, Heidegger was the contemporary philosopher who made the greatest impact on the formation of an entire generation of Spanish intellectuals. In 1930, Gaos heard Heidegger's name for the first time, when Ortega mentioned it at the headquarters of the *Revista de Occidente*. Gaos was struck by Ortega's observation: "With Heidegger, philosophy comes home to us." From that day on, Gaos understood that one must come to terms with Heidegger. For Gaos, the true critical confrontation occurred in 1933, during his first year of teaching in Madrid. By 1933, Zubiri had completed two years of study in Freiburg with Heidegger, and from supporter of phenomenology, he was converted to the philosophy of existence. Starting from 1933, and for about twenty years thence, Gaos took up existential thought as his own philosophical horizon. In the *Confesiones*, Gaos summarized his complex relationship with Heidegger's philosophy:

> As for Heidegger . . . this is what I have to say. At least during the years that I studied Heidegger under Zubiri's guidance, Zubiri interpreted the German philosopher in the sense that the nucleus of his philosophy was the truth as essence of the human being, conceived as *lumen naturale*, the human being, that is, not God. I do not recall that Zubiri discerned in Heidegger the nihilism that generally has been seen in him. Instead, I can

furnish a full explanation in the sense in which he goes into his "religación" of the human being, expounded in the essay, "En torno al problema de Dios."[41] I, however, quickly surrendered to the negative interpretation, which ends up by making Heidegger out to be a nihilist. This interpretation reached me from all sources: from the first German and French expositions and criticisms that I read, by Frederick Henry Heinemann, August Messer, Georges Gurvitch, up to those that reached me in Mexico, or were produced in America, by Alphonse de Waelhens and Alberto Wagner de Reyna. Then, little by little, as I intended to write a commentary on *Sein und Zeit*, I tried to understand Heidegger historically. Thus, I came to appreciate two points of capital significance: first, Heidegger's genealogy is not the one imposed by the four Gospels or by the Acts of the Apostles; second, the sense of his analysis of "Being-there" is not the negative one, condemned in the Epistles of the Apostles or in the Apocalypse.[42]

Having completed in Mexico the Spanish translation of *Sein und Zeit*[43] that he started in Madrid, Gaos, at long last, began to distance himself from the nihilistic interpretation of Heidegger's thought. Probably, he was influenced by Zubiri's reading of Heidegger. But, before Gaos became familiar with the *Über den Humanismus*[44] (Letter on Humanism), he interpreted *Sein und Zeit* in a special way. Its intent to explain ontology by means of subjectivity is neo-Kantian. The treatment of relations between theory of existence and truth, and the theory of being in general, according to the transcendental method is also neo-Kantian; as is its investigation, within the subject, of the conditions of possibility for being in general and for its apprehensibility. *Sein und Zeit* remains neo-Scholastic in its supposed intent to found a theory of divine infinitude within the phenomenology of human finitude, and existentialist in its conception of transcendental subjectivity as the mortal individual. *Sein und Zeit* is, moreover, phenomenological in method and Diltheyan with regard to the conception of subjectivity as historicity.

Proceeding in another direction, Gaos's interpretation of Heidegger captures the salient traits of the influence of Scholastic philosophy on the German thinker. Gaos underscores the relationship between Heidegger and Duns Scotus, who conceived human existence as a complex of modes. I am reminded of the important role that Christian faith played in shaping the earliest phase of Heidegger's thought: to conceptualize being in general via a conceptualization of time, of *Temporalität*, meant "to conceptualize a Transcendence both as to time, and to being, which could not be, if not Divine."[45]

As a student of existentialism, Gaos uses Heidegger's works, in particular *Sein und Zeit*, as a constant reference point. What I find missing is an equally constant, critical comparison with Karl Jaspers, the other twin star of existential philosophy. Aside from Gaos's translation of Jaspers's *Existenzphilosophie*[46] into *La filosofía desde el punto de vista de la existencia*,[47] Gaos's interest in the author of *Philosophie*[48] remained sporadic. The guiding light in Gaos's meandering journey through existentialism is Heidegger.

What is chiefly missing in Gaos is the critical distinction between the problematic nature of existentialism and the problematics of the philosophy of existence. We must realize that only recently has that distinction surfaced full-blown in the historiographical discourse of our time. Certainly, the dimension of existence is essential for both existentialism and the philosophy of existence. Within the philosophy of existence, such a dimension is authentic, only if it is open to transcendence, understood as ontological possibility, never as intellectually constructible theme. Within existentialism, on the contrary, the dimension of existence exhausts itself in the very act of existing. (Even existentialism, so understood, must not be mistaken for its degenerate forms and decadent interpretations. Such interpretations evoke nostalgia for the "lowest levels of the soul," and for the existences that waste away on the streets of Montmartre, wretched victims of absinth; in sum, for those sad and sinful events that end up manifestly grotesque.) For Gaos, interpreter of Heidegger, mindful of the text of his masters, especially of Zubiri, the dimension of existence is always open to transcendence. Consequently, in the vision that Gaos elaborated of existentialism, at least during the middle period of his career, transcendence cannot be considered as alienating moment. Somewhat different is the position that he adopted in the later part of his life.

Gaos's early formation, along with the influence of Ortega, García Morente, and Zubiri, greatly affected Gaos's reading of Heidegger. Gaos was also detached from his masters in a literal, spatial, geographic sense, even before the level of ideas. A thinker who moved to a foreign country and accepted it as a second home differed from the intellectuals that remained in Spain during the aftermath of the Civil War.

In 1936, García Morente also emigrated to Paris and, later, to Buenos Aires, Argentina. And Ortega y Gasset, likewise, lived for a decade abroad, whether in Europe or in Argentina. But even if we leave out the circumstance that both thinkers returned, then, to their place of birth and died in Madrid, we can grasp the diverse ideological attitudes between Ortega, for example, and Gaos, before the exile and the dissolution of the Republican government. By outlining the range of these divergences, we gain insight into the historical-cultural climate and the private passion that inspired the Spanish intellectuals of the epoch. This is especially valuable for framing the figure and the work of José Gaos, whose intellectual evolution was connected with autobiographical events.

The maternal relatives in whose household Gaos had spent his infancy and childhood were partisans of the extreme right in Spanish politics. They did not favor simply the general agenda of "Carlismo," that is, of Don Carlos de Borbón's party; they were staunch supporters of "integrismo," the arch-conservative faction at the core of Carlism.[49] At the opposite end of the spectrum, Gaos's paternal relatives stood squarely on the side of the Spanish liberals. Gaos himself began to absorb Spanish liberalism when, in 1915, he moved to his parents' house. In recalling those years, Gaos wrote that, when he saw the early signs of an imminent political change, he considered his duty to incorporate himself into the collective action of those persons who chart the course of history. On a practical level, he settled down in a political party from the moment that he judged individual action as absolutely inoperative. Gaos selected the Socialist Party from among the Spanish parties that took up the struggle to bring about the change of regime.

In 1926, Fernando de los Ríos published a book entitled *El sentido humano del socialismo*,[50] which became famous throughout Spain. According to De los Ríos, the spirit of socialism is humanist. De los Ríos maintained that the Spanish Socialist Party might be compared to the English Labor Party. Sometime later, De los Ríos became Gaos's sponsor, when the young philosopher was admitted to the chapter of the Socialist Party in Zaragoza. With lively empathy, Gaos recalled the atmosphere of great collective emotion that marked the birth of the Second Republic in Spain (1931-1936).[51] Nevertheless, around 1933, not yet two years after the birth of the Republic, the leading intellectuals, who had reunited as a group in order to serve it, were beginning to be disappointed with the Republican experience. From Gaos's point of view, however, that disappointment seemed terribly premature, really an impatience that was historically incomprehensible in comparison with the age-old patience kept with the monarchy. As early as December of 1931, Ortega also became critical of the Republic, this despite the fact that in 1930 he had founded, together with Unamuno, Gregorio Marañón, Ramón Pérez de Ayala, and others, the "Agrupación al Servicio de la República" and had participated actively in the proclamation of the Republic. Soon, however, Ortega asked questions about the new regime and severely chastised it for its mistakes.[52] In 1936, during the first days of the Civil War, Ortega, together with other intellectuals, signed a declaration of adherence to the government of the Republic. He later withdrew into a voluntary silence, well in accord with his profound convictions about the function of an intellectual.

Whether during the early years of the decade of the 1930s, or at the moment of the defeat of the Republic, Gaos had no uncertainties or hesitations. He is not one of the intellectuals who wandered abroad between Spain and other foreign countries, or between Europe and America, and never planted roots anywhere. He is consistently among those who benevolently accepted as their own destiny the Latin American countries, where they aspired to live anew the tradition of Spanish liberalism. The Mexican government, headed by President Lázaro Cárdenas, quickly accorded full hospitality to the exiled Spanish intellectuals. Among these we find, besides Gaos, Eduardo Nicol, María Zambrano, Joaquín Xirau, Ramón Xirau, Eugenio Imaz, José Medina Echavarría, Manuel Durán, J. Serra Húnter, and L. Recaséns Siches. The exiles were encouraged to become members of the "Casa de España en México." The government's official plan was to furnish an environment in which the intellectuals could pursue their activities while the Civil War continued in Spain. Yet, already by the beginning of 1939, Gaos recognized the downturn in the course of the Civil War and understood the early signs of the Second World War. He was well aware that his stay in Mexico would last much more than a year. Mexico, then, appeared to him as a destiny that he accepted, even enthusiastically.[53] Gaos had interpenetrated South American culture to such a point that, in more than one book, he delineated its characteristics, related it to Spanish culture, and above all, lived it as his own. In this respect, we may recall among his most significant works: *El pensamiento hispanoamericano; En torno a la filosofía mexicana; Sobre Ortega y Gasset y otros trabajos de historia de las ideas en España y la América española.*[54]

During the years that followed his exile, Gaos began to reconsider, in a thematic fashion, the theoretical problem of the philosophy of philosophy, previously posed by Dilthey. In these years, he developed the idea that the history of philosophy was the only legitimate base for every possible theory of philosophy, or for any philosophy of philosophy. He was glad, then, to take full advantage of the first opportunity that the Mexican government offered him to teach his theory of philosophy and to perfect the knowledge that he already possessed. The opportunity coincided with the start of the regular courses of the Facultad de Filosofía y Letras in the Universidad Autónoma de México, during the academic year of 1938-1939.

In reconstructing his intellectual career, Gaos states:

In the Instituto de Segunda Enseñanza de León, at the Universidad de Zaragoza, I taught a philosophy that consisted fundamentally of a theory of physical and psychical, ideal and metaphysical objects, treated principally by Brentano, Husserl, Hartmann, and Scheler. However, already in Madrid, I began to explicate a philosophy of philosophy. Its final articulation was given in my early lectures in Mexico and summarized in the first part of my book, *Dos ideas de la filosofía.*[55]

Apropos of the philosophy of philosophy and its inherent themes, we should also recall the following works by Gaos: *Filosofía de la filosofía e historia de la filosofía; Discurso de filosofía y otros trabajos sobre la materia; De la filosofía; Del hombre.*[56]

In 1941, Gaos was named Professor of the Universidad de Nuevo León and of Veracruz. From 1942, he began to develop courses on the metaphysics of our life: initially, one course on publicity, totalitarianism, and technocracy; then, in 1943, a course on historicism; and in the year following, another on immanentism. The years that Gaos spent teaching in Mexico were rich in scholarly productivity and original thought. He inquired about the relations between the essence of philosophy and the essence of contemporary life. Gaos's philosophy of philosophy, starting from a phenomenology of contemporary life, requires the determination of this ultimate essence. Gaos reconsidered transcendental subjectivity through and beyond Heidegger's existential analysis. He also developed a distinctive form of philosophical anthropology. Gaos investigated next the constitutive structures that characterize the human being: these range from the hand to the factor of time.[57] This investigation would be followed by an inquiry into the essential historicity of the human being. In the meantime, Gaos expanded on the essential themes of the first course that he offered at the Casa de España en México: starting from the phenomenology of expression, he intended to arrive at the explanation of the fundamental ontologisms inherent in the moral duality of the human being. Gaos taught the course many times. Each time he enriched it with new problematical starting points and, finally, with his perspective of philosophical anthropology.

In 1969, José Gaos died in Mexico City. He had founded a "school," which was to become a point of reference for many brilliant South American philosophers of our time.

Two

THE PHENOMENOLOGY
OF VERBAL EXPRESSION

1. Introductory Remarks

In his two major works, *De la filosofía* and *Del hombre*,[58] Gaos takes up all the main theoretical subjects that arouse his interest. These subjects include existence, temporality, nothingness, and subjectivity considered afresh from the perspective of philosophical anthropology. Gaos treats them in their problematic aspects. His books combine the lectures which he completed during the academic years of 1960 and 1965 at the Universidad Nacional Autónoma de México. Let us follow by comparison the key concepts of Gaos's thought that result from the complementary nature of the two works: a nature that is thematically and methodologically suggestive.

The central idea that inspires *De la filosofía* resumes a thesis already worked out by Wilhelm Dilthey. Gaos intends to develop a philosophy of philosophy or a theory of philosophy that begins with a phenomenological given: self-conscious thought verbally expressed. His point of departure is a phenomenology of verbal expression that provides the distinctions indispensable for a correct statement of problems. For the time being, I do not want to discuss the articulate logical passages of Gaosian thought. By outlining Gaos's phenomenology of verbal expression, we can discover how it leads to a phenomenology of reason, and this, in turn, to the phenomenology of principal concepts or of categories. These concepts of existence, entity, finitude, and infinitude are treated in their possible combinations. But the cardinal categories are properly those that correlate with the "not," with nothingness and with negation. These are the categories of non-existence and of infinite entity. Gaos's intention to justify the negative categories requires posing a metaphenomenological question. He must introduce a theory of categories. In order to understand the question regarding the categories of reason, Gaos investigates the empirical subject of reason. This subject is the human being that poses the question and interrogates himself or herself. More than introducing us to an existential analysis *à la* Martin Heidegger, Gaos's observations will lead us straight to an original philosophical anthropology.

Additional evidence that philosophical anthropology is a constant in Gaos's thought appears in *Del hombre*. Here the author develops anthropological inquiry, topic by topic. He pursues a philosophy of humanity and strives for a "definition of the essence of human beings or of humankind." Such an essence resides specifically in human reason. Philosophical anthropology is presented as a philosophy of reason. Gaos uses "reason" in its original etymological sense of *ratio*, and *logos*, of "metanorm" and founding structure. Reason expresses the fundamental identity of thought and language, of speaking and thinking. Gaos considers the system of expressions as a preliminary set of tools for philosophical anthropology.

The problem of objectivization through verbal expressions is fundamental to these issues. Expressions objectify through concepts. Reflection on the process of objectivization of concepts ought to begin by classifying them. Gaos ranks concepts, as objectivizations of all objects, in a special hierarchy. The transcendental concepts of existent, existence, and non-existence belong at the top. The modal concepts of possibility, impossibility, contingency, and necessity, with the correlates of finitude and infinitude are placed one level below. Still lower come the universal concepts or categories of substance and mode. Again, this itinerary leads in a circular fashion to the human being, who as subject conceives of self and objectifies self as a subject among objects. He or she then objectifies self as subject, endowed with a subjectivity of its own kind.

I want to indicate some epistemic questions or methodological problems. In both books, the author develops a threefold level of inquiry: (1) an investigation of fundamental categories or transcendentals that departs from the phenomenological given (*dato*), from expression; (2) an investigation of the system of fundamental categories, studied and described in their relationship and their intrinsic connection; and (3) an investigation of the fundamental significate or meaning of the system of categories, or of the foundation of the system of significates or meanings.

Among methodological models, the hermeneutic-phenomenological method stands out. The reference to phenomenology means that Gaos intends to treat, not of metaphysical objects, but of phenomena. Yet the method is phenomenological,

> in the sense of the phenomenology founded by Edmund Husserl: not, however, in that of the idealist philosophy which Husserl set into motion; but instead in the freer sense of philosophies like the idealist and the realist, just as Husserl's students and other scholars understood, used, and cultivated it.[59]

To the extent that it is applied to phenomena of expression, phenomenological method requires an understanding of expressions, of what is expressed by them, and "that makes it a hermeneutic method, necessarily, of things themselves."[60]

2. Definitions

Philosophy must start from the given: from thought translated in the system of verbal expressions. This is the point of departure of Gaos's inquiry. For every philosophizing subject, the categories are first in the order of being pertaining to thought. In the order of knowledge, however, first is the given, which cannot be anything that we look for ("nada buscado"). Instead, it must be something that at the threshold of every investigation we find marked by "the evidence of the indubitability of its self-presentation, of its being-there, in itself, directly" ("con evidencia de la indubitabilidad de su darse, de su estar ahí, en sí mismo, directamente"). Interpreted in this sense, the given is the verbal expression, "the thought, conscious of itself, expressed in words."

But what does "verbal expression" mean? Here in our effort to state precisely the Gaosian polysemous terminology, we must distinguish between various phenomena, of which, at present, I can provide only a summary list. By "expressor" ("expressive sign"), we understand articulated sounds, the tone of their enunciation, and corresponding graphic signs; by "indicator" and "designator," articulated sounds and their signs; by "signifier," tone and its sign; by "utterer" or "emitter," the psychic subject of the expression. We must still distinguish between the indicated, the object, and the significate. Beside the noematic contents, a series of activities and relationships come into play within the total phenomenon of expression. This series constitutes the noetic, subjective aspect of a series of various intentional events (*Erlebnisse*). These consist of the following: (1) the act or activity of uttering, or of emitting sounds with their tone, or of writing down the corresponding signs; (2) the relation between articulated sounds or their signs and concept, or between indicator and indicated; (3) the relation between concept and object or objectivization; (4) the relation between articulated sounds, their signs, and object or designation; (5) the relation between tone or its sign and psychic state, or between signifier and significate, or signification; (6) the addressee's perception of sounds with their tone or of corresponding signs, or of indicator and designator and signifier; (7) the addressee's comprehension of concept, object, psychic state, or of indicated and objectivizer, of object and significate.

I should not neglect another important distinction linked to the expressive phenomenon. This distinction between a direct and a reflex position of expressions calls to mind the classical distinction between various types of the *suppositio*.[61] Here we have an eloquent example of how Gaos utilizes elements borrowed from the Scholastic tradition and transposes them into a renovated context. He re-elaborates the tripartition of the *suppositio*, which was proposed by the fourteenth-century Scholastics: (1) the personal supposition, *suppositio personalis* (the term stands for any signified object, for a precise individual); (2) the simple supposition, *suppositio simplex* (the term stands in place of the concept of the object, and not in place of the object directly); and (3) the material supposition, *suppositio materialis* (the term refers to the voice, or to the graphic sign, or to the group of graphic signs). Strict relations subsist between the supposition and the theory of the significate. Take, for instance, the distinction between fundamental aspects of the significate: the concept or the name employed as a term for orienting the reference and the object to which that name or concept refers. In medieval logic this distinction was expressed as between signification and supposition.

By "real supposition" or "direct position," Gaos denotes the use of expressions that designate objects; by "reflex position," he denotes the use of expressions that designate other expressions. In Gaos's terminology, "reflex position" may point to either (1) simply verbal expressions, the verbal or expressive supposition (the classical material supposition, *suppositio materialis*), or (2) the thoughts that these expressions indicate, the objects that they designate, their significate, the situations that they constitute, or (3) the subjects and their addressees. We are dealing with, respectively, (1) the cogitative or logical position, followed by (2) the objective, significative, situational, and (3) subjective types of supposition.

While in *De la filosofía* Gaos's interest was absorbed by the topics related to verbal expression, in *Del hombre* he takes into account non-verbal expressions, such as the mime. In his critical evaluation, the relations between the pragmatic sphere and the semantic sphere, as well as the distinction between thought, inner word, and outer expression, remain imprecise. Such lack of precision may extend to the relations between the graphic and phonetic dimension of language, the *vox* conditioned by temporality, and its inner matrix, which somehow constitutes its foundation in a semantic sense.

The most interesting aspect of the phenomenology of verbal expressions does not consist in their description, as they indicate objectivizing thoughts, nor as they designate objects. Instead, the peculiarity of Gaos's reflection in this respect consists in his examination of verbal expressions as signifiers of mental states, emotions, and so forth. Gaos's investigation of the relationship between the subjectivity of the expression's subject and a series of psychic phenomena, which, as mediated verbally by the expression, make up that subjectivity, is also unique. In verbal expressions, the designate is what is objectified by thought and indicated by means of expressions. More simply, the designate consists of the objects of language and thought in the strict sense of the correlates of thought. The significate is what is signified by these same verbal expressions. It lies at the base of intersubjective communication and correlates directly with a series of psychic states and phenomena.

How does Gaos distinguish a psychic state from a psychic phenomenon? The first expression is to be understood in a static sense, the second in a dynamic or kinetic sense. Prominent among psychic phenomena are the *emociones* and the *mociones*, both expressing motion. Not by accident do they have a common semantic root. The Spanish term *emoción* derives from the French *émotion*, which, in turn, comes from *émouvoir*, and this from the Latin *emovere*, a compound of *movere*. In Italian the term may be translated as *emozione*, though it also conveys the idea of *commozione* or *turbamento*, and, in general, the meaning of *sentimento*. Although at times *emoción* in Gaos is synonymous with sentiment, the term *emotion* recommends itself, since, in its root, it preserves its kinetic trait. As defined in the etymological dictionaries of the Spanish language, the word *moción*, derived from the Latin *motio/motionis*, exhibits among its meanings, the idea of action (the effect of moving or of being moved), of "alteration or inclination of the mind" or "proposition in a deliberating body." In Italian, *mociones* may be rendered also as *disposizioni* or *volizioni*. For the sake of adopting a uniform terminology, and in order to keep the kinetic sense of the word, from now on I will translate *mociones* by the expression "motions of the mind." Gaos himself, in some rare instances, adopts *movimientos del ánimo* as synonymous with *mociones*.

This is not a philological ramble. To these terms Gaos assigns a fundamental importance. In reference to such phenomena as percepts and images, we need only think of the centrality assigned to the *emociones* and the *mociones*. These terms are used often in their technical meaning of sentiments and of psychic motions, ranging from impulses to volitions or acts of the will. Specifically, emotions or sentiments, and motions of the mind, classified as elementary (not composite), are inalterable psychic phenomena. They manifest themselves with the peculiar characteristics of psychic phenomena: non-extended and with no spatial location, they do not consist in sensible qualities but in activities of their own kind. They are subjective for their respective subject and intersubjective in the perception of other psyches through mimic expression.

The nature of percepts and images differs from that of *emociones* and *mociones*. Gaos's phenomenological analysis, in this regard, stretches in a twofold direction: (1) the description and examination of the noetic aspect, that is, of perception, or act of perceiving, and of imagination, or act of imagining, and (2) the analysis of the noematic content, which consists of percept and imagined images. In a quick sketch, I can only indicate how the percept is a composite. It is a whole of sensations that are elementary physical phenomena, apperceived by means of images, relations, emotions, and motions of the mind. Yet not all these phenomena—images, emotions, and so on—express equally the apperception of sensation. Thus, the relation between sensations and images is of continuity between elements of the same species (Gaos, following Franz Brentano's path, judged even images, to be physical phenomena). However, the relation between sensations and psychic phenomena, the *emociones* and the *mociones*, happiness and sadness, attraction and repulsion, is the object of different and contrary descriptions and conceptualizations.

Images are subdivided into two kinds: (1) the reproductive and (2) the creative. As the images of something, the first reproduce, represent, copy, imitate a model; the second "combine parts of percepts or, better, parts of images that reproduce percepts."[62] The role performed by the *emociones* and the *mociones* remains fundamental: just as in perception, sensations characteristic of percepts apperceive, so in imagination, sensations characteristic of images apperceive.

The real importance of emotions and motions of the mind will become apparent when I discuss the subject's *mocionalidad*. I will treat of the complex of inclinations, volitions, and so on, of the sphere of will or, properly, of psychic activity in its kinetic makeup. Gaos understands subjectivity in a dimension that he calls "formal kinetics." He departs from the traditional stratigraphic classification, whose archetype lies in ancient Greek thought, that distinguished between three kinds of soul: the rational, the vegetative, and the sensitive. According to Gaos's formal kinetics, subjectivity is formed essentially from the sphere of *emociones* and *mociones*. More about this later.

What is the relationship between expression or its significate and the psychic phenomena which constitute that relationship? I need not consider any further the signifier, that is, the expression's tone *per se*, which may be enunciative, interrogative, exclamatory, or imperative. Instead, I will look at the fundamental psychic attitudes, relative to what is objectified in the expression by the subjects. In Gaos's opinion, no more than four groups of psychic attitudes may be distinguished: (1) the enunciative tone, expressing the state of serene contemplation or of objectivization of objects, and corresponding to what traditionally has been defined as theory; (2) the interrogative tone, expressing doubt about the existence of the object; (3) the tone that expresses exclamation or wonder—with preponderance given to wonder—which is analogous to (4) the imperative tone, expressing the will to command or the will of the object's existence.

Is this classification of tones expressing *emociones* and *mociones* (emotions and motions of the mind) exhaustive? Which criterion establishes this classification? According to Gaos, strict relations subsist between the enunciative, interrogative, and wondering tones, and what they signify: theory, doubt, and wonder. Gaos recalls how in a famous passage in Book A, Chapter Two of Aristotle's *Metaphysics*, wonder is considered the origin of philosophy, while doubt and theory are related essentially to wonder:

> Philo-sophia, love of wisdom, of theory, of knowledge from and through causes and first principles, originates from wonder about something, the causes or first principles and the state contrary to the birth of wonder: a state of not wondering at anything, where the first principles and causes are known. Wonder, doubt, and theory, wonder, interrogation, and enunciation integrate thus into a complex which may be called a "theoretical complex."[63]

In opposition to this theoretical complex arise the voice and the will to command, that is, *praxis* and *poiesis*. On the other side, relegated to confused limbo, the sphere of *pathos* emerges.

At the conclusion of his phenomenology of verbal expressions, Gaos indicates the leading thread of his analysis. The theme of his discourse is the fundamental distinctions between objects and subjects and between individuals and concepts. Such distinctions stand in relations as strict as they are complex.

The distinction between individuals and concepts is presented as a division among objects. However,

> the distinction between objects and subjects lies in the relationship of opposition—an "ob-ject" of its own kind. This is a unique relationship between objects and one part of them, which are individuals. For subjects are characteristically psychic substances. Even if they possess a body, they are formed of psychic modes.[64]

A more complete examination of these relations forces us to consider objectivization in terms of the passage from objects to existents. It does not matter whether phenomenological analysis reduces objects to the physical phenomena of percepts and images, to psychic ones of emotions and motions of the mind, or to ideal phenomena of thoughts and metaphysical objects, represented by thoughts and images.

Three

THE PHENOMENOLOGY OF CATEGORIES

1. The Theme of Existence

Gaos accords primacy to phenomenological reduction. He also gives us the opportunity to come face to face with things themselves. The Gaosian "methodological" journey moves from the classes of verbal expressions to the classes of objects, given by those same verbal expressions.

Some preliminary clarifications focus on the meaning of "object" and "objectivity." Gaos understands "objectivity" as the essence of the object, just as existence is the essence of the existent. When studying objects we must not overlook what is essential: the study of the essence of the object, the "whatness" in which the object-being consists. Gaos grapples with the problem of what makes the object an object. This is the problem of the foundation (*Grund*, as the Germans would call it) of the object's objectivity. How does Gaos's inquiry on objectivity come about? Does it evolve from the relationship between the representation and the represented object; or from the investigation of the possibility of the object in general? For Gaos, the questions of objectivity and existence are the same. Expressions objectify, via concepts. As objectifiers of all objects, concepts are arranged in a special hierarchical order. Uppermost are the transcendental concepts of existent, existence, and non-existence. To clarify the sense of these transcendentals is to give a phenomenology of the categories.

The polysemous nature of expressions like "existent," "being" or "ens,"[65] and "existence" induces us to make some preliminary clarifications concerning Gaos's terminology. By "existent," which replaces "being" or "to be," Gaos means either "an existent" as a particular existent of the transcendental or "the existent" as a substantial transcendental. He adopts the Scholastic sense of "transcendental" as something that transcends the diversity of the kinds (genuses) in which things are distributed, instead of the strict existential sense as "every disclosure of Being as the *transcendens*."[66] Consequently, "being" must mean whatever in a particular existent, whether an individual or a concept, is neither its bare-bones existence nor the pure modality that resides in it. Gaos states:

> In reference to a human being, "being" does not mean simply "rationality" or "rational animality"; instead, it signifies its entire body here and now. We must entertain an abstraction from the pure or bare presence, here-and-now, to this or that subject. Being encompasses a particular heterogeneous plurality and the substantial transcendental of all such.[67]

Moreover, for "existence," we assume the particular existence, whether individual or distributed, of each existent, and also the transcendental of these existents.

I do not want to evaluate particular questions, such as the distinction between specific existence and generic existence, or on what basis the existent is the individual of a species or of a genus. Activity or being an active mode expresses the special connotation of existence. According to Gaos,

> substantive existence is the second substantiation of a first, which is the infinitive "to exist." Existence is an activity. It is the active mode designated by the forms of the modes that are distinguished from the infinitive of the active intransitive verb "to exist." Existence is designated as an active mode, as an activity of every existent: every existent exists, fulfilling the activity of existing, just as an existent who loves fulfills the activity of loving. The expression "to fulfill" is quite a designator and connotator of the activity of existing! This mode is modalized mainly by finite or infinite. . . . A mode is what it is insofar as it is a mode of an original substance or of a substance by substantiation, or else as it is a mode of the remainder of a substance. Substance is the existent and the remainder of this, the being. Existence becomes objectified as active mode of the being in every existent. The relationship implied between existent and being is a correlative of the distinction between them both. Such a relationship poses the classical problem of the distinction between essence and existence. We can resolve this issue by examining the modalization of existence as finite or infinite. Here three or four relationships must not be conflated: (1) the relationship that is existence itself; (2) the relationship of this relationship (the one between existence and being); (3) the correlation of the relationship between existence and being, along with (4) the distinction—which is also a relation—between both of them.[68]

This extensive quotation indicates the terminology or the semantic field at Gaos's disposal. The passage also heavily underscores the importance he accords the theme of existence. Prevailing over every other question, including the question of being[69]—by now ambiguous, originating from the polysemous nature of the term "being"—is the question of existence. "Existence" includes its epiphany as relation, active mode, mode of being, or mode modalized by finite or infinite. The question of existence, as a transcendental essence of the existent, lies at a crucial crossroad.

In pursuing Gaos's line of inquiry, I need not establish relationships with other prominent exponents of existentialism. I will not ask how close Gaos's thought comes to Heidegger's idea of existence as being of Being-there. Instead, I will ask why the question of existence represents an obligatory point of departure. The *what* of the investigation, the investigated, cannot be disjoined from the *how* or the way in which the what is investigated. In Gaos's thought, the how is not really a method of ontological phenomenology or of hermeneutic ontology. Gaos's method is phenomenological. The Gaosian point of departure is indicated in the given, which is thinking directly conscious of itself as expressed verbally. The given presents itself as objectivizing. The examination of what is objectivized by expressions via concepts consists in the examination of the essence of objects, of their objectivity. The examination of objectivity leads to the theme of the existence of existents. Take an object present to the thought that objectivizes it. Isn't that object an existent? This question suggests the possibility of existents neither present nor objectivized. Is existence independent of objectivity or presence? Presence may be merely a gnoseological[70] criterion of existence. Or it may be something else.

Our point of departure has been narrowed down to the phenomenology of the presence of objects, of presence in general. Phenomenology treats essentially of phenomena. Here "phenomenon" designates neither appearance (simple apparition) nor being as such. "Phenomenon" refers to what is characteristic of being. Phenomena are not phenomenological objects. Phenomena are their objectivizations, that is, their presence—existence—appearance, disappearance, reappearance, disappearance forever. Such phenomena constitute what we may call, in a literal sense, "phenomenality."

Phenomenology by way of antonomasia studies phenomenicity or existence, not essences. The phenomenology of presence is the phenomenology of existence. The phenomenology of appearance, disappearance, reappearance, and disappearance forever has its privileged place in the phenomenology of the modalization of finite or infinite existence, or within the horizon of infinitude. Infinitude, as non-finitude, implies negation and its examination. Existence, negation, and infinitude become the central moment in the phenomenology of the categories of reason.

In my introduction to the phenomenology of presence, the relationship of identity between presence and existence will again be useful. The phenomenological-methodological habit drives us to concentrate on words and then on the question: What are "existence" and "to exist"? A plausible response is that they represent the substantivization of an active mode. In what does the activity of to exist consist? To this, according to Gaos, there can be only one answer: such activity is to be-there, to be present to a subject. A subject cannot be given without its objects. The study of existence as presence and activity examines the constitution of subjects. Such a study investigates the subjectivity that consists in objectifying thoughts. Nor are objects without subjects possible, if objects are objects of concepts ("of" in the sense of *genitivus obiectivus*) and concepts are concepts of subjects ("of" in the sense of *subiectivus*). Gaos questions the possibility of existents that may not be present to a subject. The crux of the question lies in understanding what "existent" and "existence" signify in Gaos's thought.

I should not neglect the suggestive re-elaboration of phenomenological themes. Nevertheless I must indicate Gaos's own perspective and his distance from phenomenological thought on the classification of existents. As Gaos himself put it:

> To Husserl I owe the entire phenomenology of expression, the subject matter of this course; from Brentano, Husserl, Scheler, Hartmann, and Müller I derive the classification of objects through presence. My indebtedness to these thinkers becomes apparent not so much in corrections and terminological integrations, as (1) in ideas of the type that reduce existents to percepts, images, thoughts, emotions, and motions of the mind, and to possible metaphysical existents; and (2) in the ideas relative to these, to thoughts, to other possible ideal existents, and to possible objects unique to emotions and to motions of the mind.[71]

Gaos articulates the significate of existence, as property of each existent. Besides the real phenomenal and physical existence of percepts is the real phenomenal and psychical existence of acts of thought, of emotions and motions of the mind. There is also the real existence, metaphysical, physical, and psychical, of metaphysical existents. Such existents exist "really," if they exist at all. Finally, we have the ideal existence of ideal thoughts, of the objects of pure thought, distinct from ideal thoughts, and the existence of objects characteristic of emotions and motions of the mind. Such objects and thoughts exist ideally, if they exist at all.

We now come to the special characteristics of existence. Existence and presence imply each other. Activity may be designated as the object characteristic of existence. Let us try to characterize such activity in terms of an indubitable case, as close as possible. When we affirm that this particular object—this table, for example—undoubtedly exists, we mean to say that it is present here, now, for us or for me as observer. The existence of this table is equivalent to its presence here, now, for me. The designation of presence and to be present is exactly the same as that of to exist and existence: the activity of a substance in general. In our example, the substance of the activity is this table, a substantial physical phenomenon. Its presence is characterized as the table "here," a situational term that designates the place of the subject, who affirms that the table undoubtedly exists. The table is also "now," a term that designates the present time of the subject of the situation. Gaos speaks of "this presence, the instantaneous though continually renewed and conceived as having more or less duration, or a state, of activity as what we prefer to call 'existence.'"[72] In sum, the table is present at the time and place of the subject of the situation. The subject is, essentially, "conscious of herself or himself." This proposition means that, as s/he perceives, s/he is conscious of her/his perceiving. The subject is continuously present to herself/himself in the modes of the "here" and the "now." To suppose that the table exists or is present in itself, here, now, for the subject of the situation, and that this subject is, in turn, present in herself/himself, here and now, for herself/himself, means to say that presence is a relationship composed of other relationships. The relationships among the fundamental correlates—between the percept (or the phenomenon) and the situational subject, or between the subject and herself/himself—are not relations between presence and its correlates. These relations form presence itself.

Let us suppose that presence is temporal. Existents are always present to some subject. The condition for volitional activity of the conscious subject then is temporality. "Temporality" means appearance, presence, and disappearance in time or temporal modalization of existence. The conception of existence as essentially temporal activity follows from the propositions that every existence is temporal and that the concept of existing non-temporally is contradictory. But then existence reduces to real existence and ideal existents are impossible. Here lies a radical antinomy, to which I will return later on.

I have barely alluded to the nexus between presence and time. A discussion of the phenomenality of phenomena will give me the opportunity to analyze that nexus in depth. I have already commented upon the meaning of "phenomenon." The fundamental phenomenon of all phenomena is the presence of beings[73] to a subject. The concept of phenomenon may be defined on the basis of this presence. A phenomenon is understood here as every being present in itself to a subject. Such presence does not occur through the medium of a representation. Phenomena are the percepts, the images, the thoughts, the emotions, the motions of the mind, or even non-metaphysical ideal existents. Metaphysical existents cannot be understood as phenomena. Such existents are represented by the concept of metaphysical existent. I emphasize: the presence of perception, of image, of emotion, is not a mere criterion of existence. Presence is itself existence as perception, image, emotion, and so on. Besides the presence of beings to a subject, we have the presence of beings to themselves. This is the condition for the presence of other beings to the same subject.

What is the relation between phenomenon and time? At issue here is not objective time. Objective time, characterized as a homogeneous continuum, is deprived of qualitative differentiations. We are treating phenomenological time, within the horizon of possibility of an intentionally immanent consciousness. Gaos emphasizes two tenets: (1) psychic phenomena, such as emotions and motions of the mind, are intrinsically temporal; (2) every phenomenon—even physical, as in the case of images and percepts—represents an immanent temporal unity. Psychic phenomena are:

> individual in the strict sense of what the Germans call *Einmaligkeit* [once for all], the not-presenting-itself, the not existing more than once; or appearing only to disappear forever. The psychic phenomenon that returns or reappears does not do so in the rigorous sense of identity, but at the most in the sense of similarity. It is momentary in the strictest sense.[74]

The possibility of conjoining phenomenon with time requires that phenomena, such as appearance, disappearance, reappearance, and disappearance forever, appear next to the presence of beings to the subject. The subject lasts within the limits of momentariness or instantaneity. These intrinsically temporal phenomena develop in a determinate time. Such phenomena present themselves as processes, instantaneous or less so. On a par with presence or existence, they are active modes or modes of being.

We have two ways of describing these phenomena: (1) the passage from inexistence to existence (the creation from nothing to the totality of the existent is incomprehensible); and (2) the annihilation of existence. What is intriguing is the use made of the two ways of interpreting appearance and disappearance in terms of the existence of the beings or of the presence of beings to a subject.

Again, the point of departure is a phenomenological given: the unity of consciousness that intentionally embraces the temporal *ek-stasi* (ecstasies) of the past, of the present, and of the future. In Husserl's terms, temporal extension takes shape in a continuity of act. Such continuity expresses itself as remembrance, perception, and expectation. Temporal extension emerges immanently in the consciousness that relates the now having past to the now present, and to the future:

> Uniquely all that we are phenomenologically in the present moment, we are in the consciousness that is indicated as internal perception. We can only be in memory all that we were phenomenologically a moment ago. We are not yet but can be in foresight all that we will be phenomenologically a moment from now. These successive, moment-to-moment appearances and disappearances of the totality that we are in our internal perception we interpret as modes and phenomenal substances. The passage from inexistence to existence and *vice versa* may be either a creation or an annihilation. Self-consciousness is consciousness of self as (1) an existent unique in every successive present; (2) inexistent in every present immediately preceding and again (3) inexistent in every present immediately following. Or self may be understood as (4) an existent unique in the nook of the actual present, between an indefinite past inexistence and an indefinite future inexistence.[75]

These observations differ greatly from the phenomenological consciousness of time, elaborated by Husserl, for example, in the *Zeitvorlesungen*, published in Göttingen. For Husserl, it is the present that "stretches out" and encompasses the immediate past and what is expected as future. In Husserl's perspective, intentional movement broadens the present in both directions, toward the past and toward the future. Such movement arranges the continuous withdrawal of primary memory into the past that weakens until it disappears. The special quality of Gaosian reflection is not the pure observation of the now-point that appears as present moment between past and future. For him, the present and presence as a limit between the sphere of not-being-any-longer and not-being-yet is presupposed for the joining of (1) presence or existence with (2) activity. The active character of existence averts the danger that, on the ontological level, being can be negated from the moment that everything passes from one state of non-being to another. Existence lies between two inexistences, between what is no longer and what is not yet. It is not merely "consciousness of the finiteness of one's own existence—a presenting the finiteness of one's own presence to one's self. Nor is it consciousness of finiteness *sui generis*: the consciousness of an existent whose boundaries are so close, one to the other, that they press, torment or distress him, in the edge of the present . . . between the boundaries of birth and death." To exist is "to re-exist, to resist, the two collateral nothings, in an effort to survive between them."[76]

Besides presence, only appearance and disappearance must be regarded as phenomena. The continuous creation and annihilation of our existence are only interpretation of phenomenal appearance and disappearance.

2. Negation

The principal objectives of the phenomenology of the categories of reason are the description and analysis of concepts. These concepts include existence and entity, finitude and infinitude, considered in their possible combinations. The cardinal categories are correlated to the not, to nothingness and to negation. These are the categories of non-existence and infinite entity. Let us move from the categories of reason to the so-called negative categories. In these we begin to meet, "paradoxical though it may seem, what are the most lofty and most profound categories of reason."[77]

Let us consider the negative category of inexistence. The importance of negation has been frequently highlighted during the course of Western thought. Especially during the post-Hegelian period, existential philosophies stressed the significance of the negative. Systematic-phenomenological self-questioning of the phenomena of negation remains fundamental in Gaosian philosophical thought.

Some preliminary clarifications will help us to understand Gaos's position. The importance assigned to the negative and the emphasis placed on the dialectical movement of negation surely delineates a boundary zone between the Gaosian phenomenology of the negative categories and the Hegelian phenomenological conception of negation. But we are treating of a closeness-farness for a twofold reason. (1) Gaos reads a Hegel reformed, reconsidered on the basis of a modernized reading from the perspective of existentialist philosophy. (2) Gaosian phenomenology differs greatly from the phenomenology which understands as absolute truth the process that, passing through opposites, unifies them. More than to the overcoming of opposition and contradiction, more than to redemption from perishableness and negation, in sum, more than to the outcome, we must direct our attention to the process *in fieri*. This is where the cardinal categories refer to their negation.

Gaos's systematic phenomenological itinerary intends to proceed from the phenomenology of "the not" to the phenomenology of nothingness. "Nothingness" expresses the superlative case of the negation of the existence of every existent. We need to ask ourselves if, and in what sense, "the not" expresses a fundamental limitation of existence. "Not" denotes the implicit exclusion of possibility, always present in existential choice. I will move beyond selecting analogies with the idea of the *Nichts*, as fundamental fault of existence, which is expressed in some paragraphs of Heidegger's *Sein und Zeit*.[78] I will show how the concept of the not, the negative, may be correlated with the theme of temporality. Negation is the condition of the possible construction of an immanently temporal horizon. We can consider the phenomena of appearance and disappearance in the passage from inexistence to existence, or *vice versa*. As relative mode of the presence of beings, existence is in essential correlation with other phenomena through antonomasia: the appearance, disappearance, and reappearance of beings. Let us suppose that appearances and disappearances can be conceived as relations between a previous inexistence and a posterior existence. Such relations may also occur between a previous existence and a posterior inexistence. The "not" of non-existence, of in-existence must then include a dimension that is intrinsically temporal. More about this later.

When introducing the theme of negation, Gaos distinguishes between negative and negation. The contrast is between what implies a negation, that is, excludes a possibility, and what designates the act of negating and the content negated, that is, the negative proposition. It is no accident that from affirmative or positive expressions, the phenomenology of verbal expression passes to negative expressions. Gaos does not fully agree with Brentano's and Husserl's conception of negation as an act that denies a representation or an idea. Gaos's thinking is much closer to the classical conception of negation as a negative proposition. Such a proposition expresses both the act of negating and the negated content. Gaos's negative proposition coincides with Aristotle's "statement which divides something from something."[79] The negative proposition separates two concepts or removes them, one from the other. During the course of my exposition, the implicit reference to Aristotelian doctrine that is filtered through the Scholastic legacy of Thomas Aquinas and Francisco Suárez will become evident. This doctrine illustrates how in the proposition the combination of the terms expresses the combining or dissociating action of the intellect. Such an action follows the combination and dissociation of existing things.

Gaos recognizes that, beyond the negative proposition or the verbal negation, other modes of negation exist. These modes include the practical and the mimic, expressed through acts, deportments, and behaviors. Yet the phenomenology of the negative categories of reason (since the *primum* is "thought conscious of itself, expressed verbally") must begin with the description and analysis of verbal negation. The phenomenology of the not examines the question: With what parts of speech is it possible to construct the not? Here we are not treating of conjugating grammar and negation. Yet to say that "This sheet of paper is not yellow," is not to say: "I deny that this sheet of paper is yellow."[80] Constructed as an adverb of the copula, the "not" of the first expression connotes a concept that modalizes the activity of relation. Such activity is signified by the copula itself. The "I deny" in the second expression is instead constructed as an active, transitive verb. This verb has as its object the proposition introduced by the conjunction "that." The "I deny" connotes the objectifying concept of an activity that modalizes me, the subject who does the denying. With the "not," I am denying the property of yellow, attributed to the sheet. With the "I deny," I am saying that I deny. The "I deny" is a negative expression of the designator, denominator, or objectifier of the activity of denying.

I will omit Gaos's detailed description of the expressions that designate negating. Such expressions include substantives, qualifying adjectives, and negative verbs. I will also exclude Gaos's discussions of the non-designative expressions of negation, such as adjectives and definite pronouns, adverbs of time and place, negative prefixes, and the adverb of negation. What is valuable is the central motif of Gaos's original phenomenology of the not. "Not" can be constructed with all the parts of discourse. But these constructions are reduceable to two: (1) the relative not and (2) the active not. In the first case, (A) "not" denies the relations connoted by the verb "to be," or else (B) "not" is constructed with articles, definite adjectives, impersonal pronouns, adverbs, prepositions, and conjunctions. In reflexive mode "not" denies relations indicated by the relation between predicate and copula. In the second case, the active "not" denies

> the activities designated by verbs in their personal forms. These verbs include "to be" in its existential construction and its synonyms. The "not" that denies existence can be partial or total. It is partial when it denies the existence of one existent only or of more or less existents. Where all existents are negated, the "not" is total: "God is not," or "does not exist," or "There is no God"—"not nothing-exists." "Nothing" is the negative concept of the existence of all existents, of the existing, substantivized in its own unique way.[81]

When beginning the phenomenology of nothingness, Gaos emphasizes again the relations between "nothing" and the parts of speech. "Nothing," as in the case of "not," may be constructed with all the parts of speech. Let us examine the theme of nothing as negation of the existence of existents. How is it possible to deny? Or, how is the denial of the existence of existents given? To respond to these questions, I must review the ideas developed in *Del hombre*. Let us begin with Gaos's survey of the reciprocal implication between existence and presence.

Existence is equivalent to the presence of a phenomenon or being, here, now, for me. Existence as presence designates the activity of a substance in general. We now want to understand the denial of the presence of phenomena. Such presence may be in itself, or represented as present. The concept of presence comprises the important phrase, "for or to a subject, a subject present for or to itself." The represented presence is such for or to a subject, represented, in turn, as subject of presence. To understand the negation of the presence of phenomena, thought in function of appearances, disappearances, reappearances of percepts, I must specify that we are treating of denials of presence to a subject. The subject may be present or represented.

Again, the analysis of the denial of presence must begin by denying the presences designated by verbal expressions. These expressions become converted from affirmative to negative by inserting "not." We can deny an affirmative expression that designates the presence of a being. Let us consider the negative expression, "This table does not exist," or "It is not present." Thus formulated, this negation contains a peculiarity. It is contradictory. For with "It does not exist," or "It is not present," I deny what I affirm with "this." The "this" affirms the close presence of this object in itself, as percept or phenomenon, here, now, in the present, to me.

But it is not enough to affirm the contradiction of the negation of the present or represented presence. We must trace the conditions for negations without contradiction. Presences can be denied either (1) in regard to the place of the presence, here, but at a time, different from that of the presence; or (2) at the time of the presence, but in a place different from that of the presence; or (3) in a place and at a time, different from those of the presence. Is it still possible to deny, without contradiction, presence with respect to both the place and time of the presence itself? To respond to this query, I must go a step further: from the presences denied to their denial. I will begin with the existential "not." Gaos is convinced that the expression "not" indicates a concept.

> Suppose that "not" did not indicate any concept. There would ensue such a heterogeneity between "not" and the affirmative verbal expressions, all indicating single concepts or thoughts, that "verbal expression" as applied to affirmative expressions and to "not," would prove an egregious equivocation. In that case, "not" would not be a verbal expression.[82]

But there is more. The existential "not," the negation that denies existence, is a concept that includes analytically, or *a priori*, beyond its specific sign, negation itself, another negation. The negation that denies existence includes what is denied by it. The expressions "It does not exist," "not present," and "inexistent" are then pleonastic. The concept of existence or of presence is comprised *a priori* in the concept "not":

[T]he concept understood, analytically and synthetically, for "not" and for this "not" itself, these expressions do not denote any object or any presence distinct from themselves. Nevertheless with these, we can connote the presence, present and/or represented, of this and this other being, of presence simultaneous to the one conceived by means of the "not"; yet in a place distinct from the place of "this presence," either "anterior" and/or "posterior" or *vice versa*, with respect to the presence conceived through the "not," correlatively, as "posterior" and/or "anterior," or *vice versa*.[83]

To return to my question: What is the condition for negation free of contradiction? (1) A first condition is what may yield a presence distinct from the present and from the represented: a presence purely conceived as denied or comprised in the concept "not." (2) A second possibility is what is required for the appearance and disappearance of the present. An intrinsically temporal horizon is necessary for negation. Appearance and disappearance are presented as activities of substances that are percepts. Such percepts are modalized by the relation of presence. For this reason, they appear as activities. A correlate of presence is the present, which appears and disappears. Another correlate is the subject of the presence, that pure activity which is the psychic modes.

"To appear" is equivalent to "to begin to be present in any place, or to exist after not being present in any place or after not existing." "To disappear" is equivalent to "ceasing to be present in any place or ceasing to exist because of not being present in any place or because of not existing." To appear and to disappear may be denoted as creation and annihilation. Let us suppose that non-presences are thought in function of appearances, disappearances, and reappearances. These activities are conceived as displacements of percepts or as denials of presences to a subject. How then could a presence distinct from the present and the represented be possible? Such a presence would be purely conceived as denied or as comprised in the concept "not." Is there a contradiction in Gaos's themes? Gaos himself attempted an answer: the concept of presence must include the essential characteristic, "for or to a subject." A concept deprived of this characteristic cannot be the same concept of presence but another. This is the concept of metaphysical existence. But aren't we attempting to think an extreme limit? A limit, which cannot be easily compressed within a conceptual scheme, may be connoted quickly as the negative. The importance of negation and of the negative will emerge with greater clarity in the meta-phenomenological problems of Gaos's theory of the categories.

Four

FROM PHENOMENOLOGY TO THE THEORY OF CATEGORIES

1. Being and Existence in Relation to Finitude and Infinitude

Let us suppose that philosophy is a *logon didonai*.[84] Philosophy is a "giving a reason" for the existence of the existent. The questioning that produces philosophy and treats the existence of the existent should develop from the ancient questioning about being. Such questioning has its problematic foundation in the *logos*.

Existence is the proper object of philosophy. *Logos* or *logia* then must be the science of existence. We now leave our examination of the phenomenology of phenomenality to investigate the meta-phenomenological and problematic nature of the theory of the categories. We must give a reason for the original *logon didonai*.

Why justify the existence of the existent? This question does not lead us into a circle of infinite reflection. On the contrary, it brings us close to the threshold of metaphysical questioning that resounds from Gottfried Wilhelm Leibniz to Martin Heidegger: "Why being and not nothing?" We must justify the existence of the existent because of the implicatory relationship between the existent and the non-existent. Inexistence (and the negative or negation) reveals itself as a more radical and decisive object of philosophy than does existence. To the gnoseological priority of inexistence over existence, we could give another configuration: without me-ontology,[85] there would be no ontology.

In a "repetition" of sorts, which increases our uncertainty, we will reconsider the questions of existence and inexistence. Let us start from the relationships between being and existence. Gaos considers the concepts "existent," "being," and "existence" as transcendentals in the Scholastic sense of predicaments of the real. For the Scholastics, the predicaments transcend the diversity of the genuses into which things are distributed. In a broad sense they "objectify any existent, whether individual or concept, substance or mode, physical or psychical, real or ideal, phenomenal or metaphysical."[86] The concepts "existent," "being" (*ens*), and "existence" are analogous in as many strict senses as there are species of presence or activity. All that implies the concept "existence," understood in a broad sense. "Existence," in a strict sense, must be understood solely as existence of real beings or existents, such as percepts, thoughts that are psychical acts or phenomena of consciousness, emotions and motions of the mind. Is the existence of metaphysical beings purely ideal? Rather than distinguishing between real and ideal existence, Gaos prefers speaking of existence in a broad sense and then specifying it as percept, image, or as metaphysical being.

But we must reconsider the question of existence and of inexistence. We will begin with the relation/distinction between being and existence. This relation is of such importance that it supplants the traditional distinction between essence and existence, on which the Scholastic philosophers have so greatly insisted. But more: for Gaos, the differentiation between being and existent is concealed in the classical distinction between essence and existence. What remains to be seen is whether the question can be put in these terms.

In Thomas Aquinas's thought, essence is one thing, existence another. According to the Thomistic vision, where the urgent need for the unity of being prevails, existence cannot also be considered as pure accident. Even if essence and existence coincide only in God, pure act and most perfect being, and remain distinct in every creature, existence is still not mere accident. Existence is instead the actuality (*ultima actualitas*) of essence. Existence refers to essence as does act to potency. A different discussion is whether Francisco Suárez, who also earned great renown in the tradition of Spanish thought, let the real distinction between *esse per essentiam* and *ens per partecipationem* slide into the modal distinction between God, *ens necessarium*, real in Himself, and creature, *ens (per aliud) possibile*. What intrigues me here is whether the distinction between essence and existence is the same distinction, not yet fully clarified, between being and existence; or, better, whether the distinction between being and existence may be identified with the distinction between essence and existence.

We must distinguish between two different levels: between (1) a historiographical reconstruction of the matrixes of Gaosian thought, or of its relation with tradition, and (2) Gaos's special theoretical perspective. He asserts sometimes that existence, as ultimate act, is "the real existence of that which, without it, would be purely ideal."[87] But is this ultimate act (*acto último*) the *ultima actualitas* of Thomistic thought? Or instead do some other and fundamental components come into play that reconnect to contemporary *Existenzphilosophie*? According to contemporary thought and Gaos, existence appears as "ex-sistence" (*ex-sistentia*) in its developing from a spatially and temporally circumscribed situation. Emerging from pure presentness, existence is an impulse and a yearning toward transcendence. Existence is the "in-between" (*Zwischen*) or the bridge between being and being-there.

I am not engaged in drawing attention, at all costs, to the novelty of Gaosian reflection. The historiographical undertaking is not what interests me. Nor am I picking out and enumerating points of convergence and divergence with outstanding exponents of the philosophy of existence. Like a bridge thrown between being and being-there, existence is revealed as an entryway, at times accessible, at other times inaccessible, and at yet other times, leading inexorably to loss and shipwreck.

In view of the complexity of the theoretical components of Gaos's thought, I am interested, instead, in assessing the special meaning that he attributes to the concept of existence. As a consequence, I want also to evaluate the variation between the Scholastic distinction of essence and existence and the distinction of being and existence. The specific difference between both distinctions is given by the special relationship that Gaos instituted between existence and inexistence. The Gaosian relationship presupposes and implies an immanently temporal horizon. On the contrary, in the Thomistic distinction between essence and existence, the question of time is excluded in the sense indicated by existentialist thought.

Gaos asks whether it is possible to distinguish being and existence on the basis of another criterion. Is it possible to separate a being and its existence or its presence? Doubtless, such a distinction is not always possible. The appearances and disappearances (*apariciones y desapariciones*), present in the phenomenology of "phenomenality" may be interpreted either as "displacements" (*desplazamientos*) of phenomena, or as creations or annihilations (*creaciones o aniquilaciones*); in other words, as existence in relation with nonexistence. But, let us suppose that being is conceivable as inexistent. Moreover, it is possible to distinguish being from existence. Inexistence is, then,

> the separation between existence and being. It is the non-simultaneous presence of being and existence, the presence of being for itself only or without existence . . . presence uniquely in thought. For an inexistent being can be present uniquely in thought or not present outside of thought. With this clarification we remove, if not the contradiction, at least the paradox of a presence of inexistence, the presence of the not present.[88]

So far, we have barely indicated that the existence/inexistence relation represents the entrance hall to the question of temporality. Existence, in relation to inexistence, may be conceived in two ways: either temporally or non-temporally. From the temporal perspective, there exists either an existence posterior and/or anterior to inexistence, or an inexistence anterior and/or posterior to existence, as when appearances and disappearance are interpreted, respectively, as creations and annihilations. Besides this typically Gaosian way of conceiving existence, we could interpret in a non-temporal key the relationship of existence with inexistence. Indeed, if time is a mode and not a substance, it cannot be put either before or after the existent. To surmount this difficulty, the existent itself has been represented as inexistent or as plain nothing. We have tried very hard to think of an existence without relationship—whether temporal or of any other kind—with inexistence. We have tried to think of a pure existence. Then, existence between inexistence, existence in relation with inexistence, would be finite existence. Existence without any relationship to inexistence would be pure or infinite.

We now face the problem of the relation between two forms of existence and being, finite and infinite. Are both forms of existence possible for any being or do they require, respectively, a finite being and an infinite being? Let us suppose the existence of a finite being of finite existence and an infinite being of infinite existence. We deny the existence of a finite being of infinite existence or an infinite being of finite existence. Let us grant a biunial correspondence between the finitude and the infinitude of being and the finitude and infinitude of existence. We still must understand infinite existence and the connection between finitude and infinitude. We stand at the threshold of the problem of giving a reason for the concepts of inexistence and infinitude, of the negative categories, and of negative reason. Finitude and infinitude are the presuppositions, the tasks, the questions, for posing the fundamental question of philosophy: the question about itself. We must not forget the importance of the conception that originated with Wilhelm Dilthey, the conception of philosophy as philosophy of philosophy. More about this later.

As for now, my interest is, strictly, "to punctuate just what are the finitude and the infinitude that cause the distinct existents, the diverse beings and existences, to be finite or infinite."[89] My point of departure is the consideration that finitude and infinitude are pure concepts of relative modes. Passing from the phenomenal level to the metaphysical one, I will treat of the strict logical correlation between the concepts of finite and infinite. Neither of these concepts will be conceivable without the other. To fully comprehend the relation of finite and infinite, as pure concepts of relative modes contradictorily correlated one to the other, means to confront the broader problem of the antinomies.

2. The Antinomies

I will try to establish, in a preliminary fashion, whether finitude and infinitude exist in a relation of contradiction. We will see how only with questioning the finite/not-finite antinomy, can we arrive at the *raison d'être* of the fundamental categories of reason. These categories include in-existence, in-finitude, and *raison d'être*, which is the essence of philosophy.

Philosophers are familiar with Kant's treatment of the antinomies in the "Transcendental Dialectic" of the *Critique of Pure Reason*: in the attempt to go back from the objects conditioned by the senses to their unconditioned cause, that is, to the total series of their conditions, human reason falls into antinomies. By virtue of its own processes, reason comes into conflict with itself. No need to dwell on the Kantian treatment of the antinomies inherent in rational cosmology. I will not consider the doctrine that has as its object the idea of the world. This idea is born from the illegitimate attempt to apply the categories to themselves, in other words, from the reflexive use of the categories. My main interest lies in the antithesis of pure reason in Gaos's own reflection. Taking up *en bloc* Kant's first two antinomies, Gaos observes:

> Finitude or infinitude, by addition or division of the world in space and time, constitute Kant's first two antinomies. This means that at least some

correlative finitudes and infinitudes stand in relation to the concept of antinomy.[90]

In fact, "all the Kantian antinomies would be, then, more or less fundamentally, antinomies of finitudes and infinitudes." Nevertheless, "not all antinomies reduce to the Kantian ones, nor do all finitudes and infinitudes reduce to those of the Kantian antinomies."[91]

I want to see if all the Kantian antinomies may be considered, as Gaos thinks, antinomies of finitudes and infinitudes. The antinomies of reason correspond to the four groups of categories already described in Kant's *Transcendental Analytic*. These categories are grouped according to quantity, quality, relation, and modality. They present an internal articulation that confers on each antinomy its special character. If we understand the antinomy between the finite and the infinite in a purely quantitative sense, Kant's antinomies are not all of finitudes and infinitudes. In a broader sense, the contradiction between finite and infinite occurs in all four antinomies. In the first two antinomies Kant poses the thesis of the finite and the antithesis of the infinity of the world. He also presents the thesis of the world's non-divisibility and antithesis of its divisibility *ad infinitum*. In the last two antinomies, the finite/infinite contradiction appears. This contradiction pertains no longer to the structure of the phenomenon but to its origin and existence. Gaos correctly points out that, in the fourth Kantian antinomy, the postulate of a necessary and noumenal, or metaphysical existent derives from presupposing an infinite existence. The finite taken together with a being capable of infinite existence is incomprehensible.

Gaos is well aware of the complex problematic nature of the antinomies. He knows that the conflict between thesis and antithesis can be read as between dogmatism (or rationalism) and empiricism. From a theoretical point of view, neither rationalism nor empiricism can prove their assumption, since their demonstrations neutralize one another in turn. In order to remove the causes of the antinomies, we must distinguish phenomena from things-in-themselves. We must also abstain from applying to phenomena the principle that the conditioned requires the totality, unconditioned by its conditions. It is not possible to find the unconditioned in the phenomenal world. It is equally impossible to find any concept of what lies beyond the phenomenal. For the attempt to conceptualize the unconditioned is equivalent to phenomenalizing the ultimate *raison d'être* of phenomena. The solution to the problem of the antinomies resides, thus, in assuming the idea of the world. This idea is considered not as reality but as a rule that stimulates the intellect to go back to the series of the phenomena, without stopping at anything unconditioned.

Once having considered the entire question of the antinomic nature of pure reason, Gaos believes it necessary to:

(1) compile an inventory of the antinomies, an inventory more complete than Kant's, which, as Hegel demonstrated, does not appear to be complete . . . (2) even without characterizing the antinomies in a more rigorous fashion, complete that characterization. The antinomies would be given a *raison d'être* more satisfactory than the Kantian one. What Kant provides is not satisfactory, because of, among other reasons, the differentiation drawn between the first two and the last two antinomies. This position is always estimated to be especially unsatisfactory.[92]

Still, Gaos does not seem to appreciate in depth that the difference between the first and the last two antinomies is *in re*. One thing is the regression from one condition to another, which was discussed in the first two antinomies. The goal of this regression is to confirm either a finitist or infinitist conception of reality. Another thing altogether is the regression discussed in the last two antinomies.

In the first group of antinomies the regression is mathematical and requires homogeneity in quantity. In the second group the regression is dynamic and permits a heterogeneous condition, extraneous to the series. In addition, I could point out the architectonic correspondence between the first two and last two fundamental propositions of pure intellect. The first two propositions are intuitive and of mathematical use. They pertain to the nature of the object or to the conditions of possible experience. The other two propositions are discursive and of dynamic use. They refer to existence or to the conditions of possible objects of experience.[93]

What interests Gaos above all is the rethinking of the antinomic nature of reason. He attempts to reduce all the metaphysical and ideological antinomies to the antinomy through antonomasia. This antinomy is between idealism and realism, which appears in the antinomy between subject and object. As Gaos put it:

> In the history of humanity as well as in an individual life, the subject has been, and still is, seen, imagined, conceived. By "subject" I mean each of us. We are the human beings here. Each of us is an existing member of the existent, a partial object or part of the total object. The Whole is objectified by each of us in every instant of the present: *voilà naïve realism.*[94]

A given throughout history is that we have been conceived "as the subject objectifier of all the objects, of the total object, of the Whole. . . . This is radical idealism." Toward the conclusion of his study, Gaos may suggest some reservations about his reduction of all antinomies to the realism/idealism or subject/object antinomy. These reservations concern the theoretical implications of his discourse. But this is a topic for another discussion.

We must understand how in Gaos's judgment, idealism cannot be resolved into empirical idealism. The idealist subject cannot be conceived as a subject that is part of the total object. The subject is the subject of the total object. To the extent that the subject transcends the total object, it is transcendental. For such a subject, it is natural "to stretch," with an intentional movement, toward the total constitution of the objects via the concepts: "the transcendentality of the subject moves toward this, toward the totality of the constitution of the objects by means of the concepts."[95]

Gaos next reviews the combinations of the terms of the antinomy, finitude and infinitude—spatial, temporal, entified[96]—of the world. He also evaluates the antinomy between subject and object. According to the realist conception, the subject that is conceived as a partial object of its total object, be it finite or infinite, cannot be conceived as great as its total object. For this reason, realist philosophies have conceived either an infinite world or an infinite God that bestowed infinitude on the total object. For such philosophies subjects are entirely finite, or existentially infinite, but not with regard to being or *ens*.[97] Otherwise, the transcendental subject can conceive its total object as finite or infinite, even though "the 'final' consequence of the totality of the constitution of the objects mediated by concepts is the identification of the infinite subject and its infinite object, in the unique absolute 'infinitist' philosophy."[98]

Four combinations between the antinomy *par excellence* and that of finitude/infinitude are possible: (1) absolute finitism[99] with finite subjects in a finite world; (2) absolute infinitism with infinite subject of an infinite world; (3) finite subjects in an infinite world, which may be divine or not, or created by an infinite God; and (4) infinite subject of a finite world. During the course of the history of Western thought, major credit has been given to the combination of finite subjects in an infinite world, or a world created by an infinite God, and to the combination of an infinite subject-object. Yet Gaos considers more coherent the combinations of finitism and absolute infinitism.

What counts is not to assert simply finitism or infinitism. I want to reach the very heart of the antinomies. I want to question how the essence of the human being consists of them. We will pass from the level of a historiographic reconstruction of the antinomies and an investigation of their complete inventory to the level of philosophical anthropology, with the recognition of the antinomic essence of humanity. The two areas are not entirely independent of one another. Together, they contribute to determine a morphology of the antinomies.

But what are the ultimate and radical antinomies? They are those that include the finitude or infinitude of being and existence. According to Gaos,

> they are the antinomies of the principal transcendental concepts, the modal and moral transcendentals, that is, infinite being and existence, either the necessary existent, or the Good; and finite being and existence, either the contingent existent, inexistence, or the Evil, above all, the inexistence of the existent (contingency, the finitude of the existent) or nothingness.[100]

To this antinomy "of concepts of metaphysical objects or existents" would be reducible "all the remaining concepts of the same class, be they concepts of the material world, or of souls and spirits, or even of infinite beings abstracted from concrete ones."[101] Let us set aside, for now, the relationships between the antinomies of concepts of metaphysical objects and the antinomies of concepts of ideal objects. These relations form a system of the two groups. I will inquire, instead, about the central motif of the "transcendental concepts, both modal and moral." To infinite being and existence and, therefore, to the necessary existent or the Good, are opposed finite existence and being, and therefore the contingent existent, either inexistence or the Evil. If the existence of the necessary existent is the good, then the inexistence of the existent is nothingness or the evil.

At first sight, the cardinal point of our orientation falls well within the Scholastic or Thomistic horizon, where the transcendentals, namely, the *Ens* and the *Bonum*, are convertible into one another.[102] But here I am not concerned with acknowledging, generically, the traditional metaphysical doctrine of the good. This doctrine identifies the good with reality or even with supreme reality. I am asking specifically: In what sense are the finitude and infinitude of existence, or existence and in-existence opposed to one another? The mainstream interpretation is formed by the cardinal modal and moral categories and the polestar by the necessity-contingency binomial. Infinite existence is defined as necessary and finite existence as contingent. Accordingly, we should read, "in a clearer light," the antinomy between finite and infinite existence as the antinomy between the contingent and the necessary.

Here Gaos's discourse becomes involved in a knot of aporemes. To infinite or necessary existence (or to the good) are contraposed non-existence (or the evil) and the inexistence of the existent, that is, the contingency or finitude of the existent (or nothingness). Are these the same concepts? Strictly speaking, contingent existence is opposed to infinite or necessary existence, the one being the contradiction of the other. Also, Gaos's definition of the inexistence of the existent as finite or contingent existence is not clear enough. What does he understand by that definition? Does he want to characterize the existential finitude of the human being? Or does he want to refer to the Kantian concept of nothingness as *nihil privativum*? Kant's quadripartition of the concept of nothingness, in the final pages of the *Transcendental Analytic*, adds the following definition of *Nichts*: "Reality is something; negation is nothing, namely a concept of the absence of an object, such as shadow, cold (*nihil privativum*)."[103] The examples indicate the sense of the contingent (*Zufällig*): contingent is any being to which it "befalls" to exist. The contingent does not have in itself the necessity of its own existence. Suppose that this is true. Moreover, the existent's inexistence, qua contingent existence, can be reduced to the Kantian *nihil privativum*. Non-existence refers then to the Kantian concept of *nihil negativum*. The *nihil negativum* is the impossible, that which is opposed to every possibility from the moment that the concept annihilates itself.

The definitions of the negation of infinite or necessary existence refer to the modal realms: non-existence to the impossible, and contingency or finitude of existence to the contingent. But, on further thought, do we mean to exclude the realm of possibility from this frame of references of the modal categories? This is an important realm for every discourse on human existence. Is finite existence, when referred to the human being, anything other than possible existence? Since Gaos, in other places, connotes contingent or finite existence as possible existence, he seems to accept this hypothesis. Yet the reducibility of finite existence itself and non-existence, respectively, to *nihil privativum* and *nihil negativum* remains open to discussion. The contradiction between finitude and existential infinitude, in all its problematic aspects, also remains unexplained. In following the development of Gaos's arguments, we need to appeal to other hermeneutic categories and to another network of conceptual references.

We must understand, beyond a purely logical-systematic reconstruction of the antinomies, the ultimate aim of Gaos's refections on the antinomic nature of reason. From the point of view of philosophical anthropology, the antinomic essence of humanity is in question. The hermeneutic horizon, where we may pose the question of human essence, must include the level of what Gaos calls the *mocionalidad* of the human subject. By *mocionalidad* he means the complex of inclinations and volitions, that is, the sphere of the will or psychic activity in general, in its kinetic constitution. My task is to show how the foundation for the logical-apophantic level of discourse may be found on a pre-categorial level. Gaos proposes to demonstrate how the antinomic nature of the metaphysical concepts is based on the pre-conceptual nature of human *emocionalidad* and *mocionalidad*. He will indicate how, from a cosmological point of view, *emocional* and *mocional* antinomic nature is the ultimate anthropological fact. Lastly, Gaos will justify his antinomic theory of the essence of human nature.

The antinomic nature of the categories of human reason, especially the cardinal concepts of God or the good, and of the nothing or the evil, consists of two specific characteristics:

(1) [S]ome concepts are contrary even to the point of being contradictory. God is the infinite existent, insofar as the pure existent or negation of every non-being. The Nothing is pure non-being. The Good is the infinite Good, insofar as pure being, or negation of every evil. The Evil is pure evil. (2) Some concepts are concepts of objects. Their existence apart from the concepts themselves can neither be affirmed nor denied, because: (A) they are not concepts of phenomena; (B) they are not concepts of objects of conclusions derived from premises, the objects of which are phenomena; (C) nor are they concepts of objects of postulates of theorems, the objects of which are phenomena. Yet a person can affirm or deny by means of an *emocional* or *mocional* choice. He or she can will the existence of God or of the Good, out of love for existents. Love motivates desire for their

boundless well-being. Or a person can will the inexistence of God or evil, out of hatred toward existents. Hatred motivates desire for their inexistence.[104]

But we need to understand: the *emociones* of love and hatred and the volitions motivated by them are not simply the cause of affirming or negating the existence of the objects of the concepts "God" and "nothingness." These *emociones* and *mociones* of desiring good and evil are the *raison d'être* by which such concepts are thought. The antinomic nature of concepts of pure reason is the effect of the radical antinomy between love and hate, good and evil. Consequently, we must look for the foundation that makes the categorial level possible on a primordial and self-justifying level. According to Gaos, if we were not capable of love or hate, we would never have thought the cardinal categories of pure reason: "if we were not the subjects of love and hate that we are, we would not be the rational beings that we are."

We are not simply replacing the priority of *cogito* with the priority of the sphere of feelings and volitions. But what does it mean to say, "We would not be the rational subjects (in the sense of pure and practical reason) that we are, if we were not the 'emocionales' and 'mocionales' subjects (moral) that we are?"[105] The antinomic nature of love and hate, of good and evil, is primordial and radical, as viewed from three angles. First, love and hate are not pairs of contrary concepts: they are motivating emotions (*emociones motivantes*), and good or evil represent the activities or modes of these motivating emotions. Nevertheless, love and hate, good and evil, are in themselves contrary in such a way that their concepts appear contradictory. Second, the antinomic nature of these *emociones* and *mociones* is radical in the sense of *radix* (root) or *raison d'être* (ground) of the antinomic nature of the concepts of reason. Third, Gaos considers the antinomic nature of love and hate, good and evil, as an ultimate fact or phenomenon, for which there is no justification. Gaos is interested in a twofold argument. (1) The essence of the human being is antinomic. Quite relevant is the fact that God is far from being the conceptual or objective reason of humanity. (2) Theology and, in general, metaphysics is not the key to anthropology. The subjective reason (*emocional* or *mocional*) for the concept of God, and for the remaining categories of human reason, resides in the moral essence of the human being. In other terms, anthropology is the passkey to both theology and metaphysics.

For Gaos, beyond or against the thought of traditional metaphysics, which holds that God is the first principle, Who justifies Self and everything else, *el hombre* is "el hecho o fenómeno último por el que da razón de todo lo demás, incluso Dios." The human being is the ultimate fact or phenomenon, by virtue of which s/he justifies everything else, God inclusive.[106] Thus, it is *el hombre* who does not need to provide a *raison d'être* for humanity.

These statements are consistent with the limits of human reason and with the finitude of the human being; in short, with the horizon of an existential hermeneutic. Still, we ask ourselves: how does Gaos manage to justify the pre-conceptual level of *mocionalidad* as the *raison d'être* of the categories of reason? Has Gaos succeeded in justifying that pure reason has its foundation in praxis? And is the pure subject the subject of love and hate, a subject that he calls pathic (*pático*)? Gaos challenges us to understand why the secret of ontology and of me-ontology must be found in the erotic and in misology. In response to that challenge, I will review the key passages of Gaos's theory of categories.

Five

THE THEORY OF CATEGORIES

1. The *Raison d'être* of the Categories of Reason

We have arrived at a fundamental crossroad of Gaosian reflection. Let us retrace briefly the journey that we have already mapped out. I will recapitulate the main points of the essential theoretical questions that have constituted the principal roads.

Our point of departure has been represented by the phenomenology of verbal expression. Gaos's fundamental idea that the ultimate and radical object of philosophy is philosophy itself is well known. Nevertheless, any attempt to define philosophy must consider how philosophy manifests itself as thought expressed verbally. Let us suppose that philosophy ought to start from the given. This given is the thought that is conscious of itself expressed verbally. For Gaosian phenomenology, verbal expression becomes polarized toward objects of concepts that are designated by expressions. Those objects are revealed as the object of the phenomenology of verbal expression.

We now understand the problem of defining the objectivity of objects. We also comprehend the relationship between that objectivity and objectifying concepts. In short, we have posed the fundamental question of existence, understood by Gaos, as "a relative mode, of presence," as "an active mode of 'being' [the *ente*, as he calls it]." "Existence" is a "mode that is conceived as finite in some beings and infinite in others, since it requires the finitude or infinitude of the respective beings themselves." We have arrived, thus, at the themes of finitude and infinitude. Their relationship is constituted by negation through antonomasia, the concept "not."

Next we examined negation in general, especially negation *par excellence*, the "not." We also investigated nothingness, understood not as abstract non-being, but as inexhaustible source of wonderment and philosophical questioning. Then a short step took us to some themes of existential thought, which with good reason has converted the adage, *nihil ex nihilo fit* (nothing comes out of nothing) into the principle, *ex nihilo omne ens qua ens fit* (from nothing comes forth every being *qua* being). Above all, we examined the negative concepts: inexistence, existential infinitude, finite existence, and infinite existence. These concepts have been understood as the chief matter of philosophy during the entire course of its history. Other problems also came to light. The concepts "not" and "inexistence" were revealed as synonymous. The concepts "finite" and "infinite" were demonstrated as related to the "not," as are all contradictory concepts. In addition, these concepts imply a "not" in the form of a negation of the negation. We consequently arrived at a crucial point: to give a reason for the cardinal negative concepts, for in-existence and in-finitude, and for the concept of providing a *raison d'être*. To give a reason for these concepts is to give a reason for human reason itself.

But what does it mean to give a reason for the concepts of inexistence, of infinitude, and, especially of the divine infinitude? We have already considered, in its general scope, the Gaosian program of providing the *raison d'être* for the cardinal negative concepts of reason. Now we must determine, more analytically and at the heart of the meta-phenomenological question concerning the theory of categories, what Gaos means specifically by "to give a reason." Does he want to attribute a necessitating character to the *raison d'être*, or to interpret it as a condition of possibility? Or instead, as it seems to me, is he seeking the foundation of the conditions of possibility for the categories of reason? And is the foundation, so understood, the same as the fundamental significate of the global system of significates?

I have often remarked on the many components that flow into Gaosian thought, from ancient tradition to contemporary influences. To recall only schematically the historical-theoretical source of the theme of the "to give a reason (*Grund*)" why a thing is what it is, is an arduous undertaking. I shall abstain from it here. Suppose we look at some central moments in the history of Western thought—not for the sake of mere digression, but in order to specify a significant *Leitfaden* (guide). We will then always find ourselves between a twofold alternative: to assign or not to assign a necessitating character to the notion of foundation.

Gottfried Wilhelm Leibniz argued beyond the Aristotelian concept of foundation as essential cause by virtue of which a thing is what it is. In the *principium rationis sufficientis* (principle of sufficient reason), Leibniz specified a connection that is not a necessary connection and yet can justify the thing. The Aristotelian notion was founded on the necessity of things, on why something cannot be different from how it is. It finds its counterpoint in a notion that is based on the possibility of the thing. Leibniz distinguished between the *principium rationis* as foundation of contingent truths and the principle of contradiction as foundation of necessary truths. Christian Wolff reduced the principle of sufficient reason to a necessary meaning. Subsequently, Christian August Crusius assigned a character of not necessary to the principle of sufficient reason. Crusius distinguished it from the principle of causality. Yet after Crusius, a causal character again was assigned to the *principium rationis*. In *Die vierfache Wurzel des Satzes vom zureichenden Grunde* (On the Fourfold Root of the Principle of Sufficient Reason), Arthur Schopenhauer considered both the principle of causality and of sufficient reason equally as expressions of the principle of necessity.

I intend to avoid a theoretical close examination of the argument in question. Here I can only call attention to one occurrence in the panorama of twentieth-century thought. Despite the lingering echo of the Cartesian *fundamentum absolutum et inconcussum*, a new model of foundation, proposed by existential thought, has been gaining ground. The foundation questions the model of Western rationality, of the traditional *logos*: the correspondence between logical necessity and necessity in the real world; or, the capacity of logical systems to describe the real. The question of an inferential and existential foundation has come to light in Heidegger's thought. A thesis that profoundly differs from the necessitating meaning of the notion of foundation is: liberty is the foundation of the foundation and hence the abyss (without bottom) of Being-there. At the base of the foundation lies the relationship between Being and Being-there, along with the rooting of Being-there in the world. From this rooting, the limitedness of essential possibilities emerges. The foundation, *qua Grund*, is *Ab-grund*, abyss and chasm, and also soil and ground of being, abysmal foundation.

As a successor to Nietzsche and Heidegger, Gaos does not assign the character of necessitating cause to the *raison d'être*. In the *raison d'être* for the negative categories of reason, he discerns the non-rational fount of reason. This ground constitutes the pre-moral origin of the moral, or the fundamental significate of the entire system of significates. Every comparison, however, with Nietzsche's "deconstructive" thought eventually will lead off our road. Starting from *Human, All-Too-Human* (*Menschliches, Allzumenschliches*), Nietzsche constructed a "chemistry of ideas and feelings," centered on the search for the simple elements of things. He also questioned how anything can be born from its opposite.

The task that Gaos proposes is characterized by a twofold purpose: (1) to account for the negative categories of reason, and (2) to account for the account itself. Let us consider the first aspect of the question. The concepts of inexistence and infinitude cannot be referred to phenomenal objects. Such concepts are thought by the human being (*hombre/uomo*),[107] who "creates them, purely and simply, because moved by love or hatred toward other existents and toward self. This is the only *raison d'être* possible of those concepts: either this reason, then, or none, and such concepts would have no reason to be."[108] I want to clarify the relationships that mediate between the metaphysical concepts of practical reason and those of pure reason and, especially, the relationship of sameness between the cardinal categories of both spheres. The equations established by Gaos between being (pure, infinite *ens* and existence) and goodness and between evil and the privation of being or not being must be examined. The *raison d'être* of the Infinite (either infinite good or God) and of inexistence (either nothingness or evil) cannot reside directly in phenomena. Can a "phenomenal" infinitude ever occur? And isn't inexistence only a way of conceiving the phenomena of appearance and disappearance?

The original fount, the secret of ontology and of the more radical me-ontology, must be sought in the realm of the erotic and in misology. The not, or negation, or limit is fundamental potency. The most profound meaning of verbal and practical negation resides in the loves and hates motivating the negative categories of reason. What other translation for "not" and "negation," if not aversion and hate? Even in a simple proposition of the type, "This sheet of paper is not white," the recognition of the inexistence of the relationship between subject and predicate expresses aversion: whence the motive to sound in greater depth the sphere of will and the emotions that exist essentially in relation to it.

Gaos considers that a human being's prerogative is to value that person's own satisfactions as goods and dissatisfactions as evils, and to will at times the ones, at times the others. Between (1) satisfactions or goods and dissatisfactions or evils and (2) will are interposed some distinctive and fundamental *emociones-mociones*: love and hate. "These are archetypically 'intentional': they are relative to the loved or to the hated." Hatred motivates willing evil for the hated person, willing his or her dissatisfaction, and even the hated person's annihilation. Such will thinks the inexistence of the hated one. The concept of inexistence is motivated by a volition, directly motivated by hatred. Love motivates willing the beloved's good, willing his or her satisfaction, and even the beloved's infinite happiness. Such volition thinks the beloved's infinite happiness. Thus, even the concept of infinitude is motivated, through a volitional act, by a fundamental *emoción-moción*: love.

The *raison d'être* of the negative concepts of reason, of inexistence and of infinitude, or the foundation of their possibility, and the fundamental significate of the global system of categories cannot reside in logic or ontology. The foundation for the categories of reason does not consist in the motionless, atemporal, and constant structure of the being of things. That categorial foundation is implicit in the sphere of subjectivity, in what most appropriately belongs to the subject. What Gaos considers the constitutively original ambit of subjectivity is the non-rational dimension of *emocionalidad* and *mocionalidad*.

We are following Gaos's course beyond the clarification of how pure reason is based upon practical reason. Gaos wants to justify both theory and praxis. He begins his argument from a primogenial place, from an original, non-conceptual fount, of a pre-logical nature: "the moral, erotic, misological, and volitional *mocionalidad*" of the human being. Gaos's reform of the notion of subject implies a "going beyond" the subjectivity of traditional thought. We need to think about this notion in order to gather the theoretical implications that a similar course of thought involves.

2. From Transcendental Subject to "Pathic" Subject

Gaos carries to conclusion the theoretical project already delineated between the nineteenth and twentieth century. The birth of the subject, characterized by originating from the sphere of affectivity, corresponds to the eclipses of the logical subject, of critical-transcendental matrix. In this sense, we may speak of crisis and transfiguration of the subject in Gaosian reflection. The crisis of subjectivity is a dominant theme of contemporary philosophical debate, especially in reference to the arc of thought from Nietzsche to Heidegger. Today by "crisis of the subject," we mean not only "a dissolution of 'modern' subjectivity." By that phrase we also understand "a dissolution of being itself (no longer structure but event, which is no longer given as principle and foundation, but as announcement and 'story')."[109] Gianni Vattimo has well characterized the co-ordinates of the problem. The crisis does not merely carefully examine the notion of subject. It questions the subjectivity of the epoch in which Nietzsche and Heidegger reflect.

Referring to the contemporary debate in outline, I can note briefly why, according to some authoritative and critical voices, the reference to Nietzsche and Heidegger is necessary. The author of *Thus Spoke Zarathustra* (*Also sprach Zarathustra*) announced the crisis of subjectivity "as an unmasking of the superficiality of consciousness." While in his more mature works,

> the unmasking of the superficiality of the self-conscious subject will proceed more and more explicitly in lock step with the unmasking of the notion of truth and with the more general dissolution of being as foundation; so much so that one can say that the completed expression of the crisis of subjectivity in Nietzsche is the announcement of "the death of God," . . . formulated for the first time in *Die fröhliche Wissenschaft* [The Gay Science].[110]

Likewise, in Heideggerian reflection, we can identify the itinerary (with its own special characteristics, when taken as a whole) that leads from the unmasking of the metaphysical subject "to the dissolution of being as foundation and to nihilism." Let us suppose that these general co-ordinates of the problem are more important than the question of "going beyond the historically destined 'essence' of metaphysical subjectivity" and the problem of going beyond metaphysics. We must now limit our observations to the theme of the transcendental subject's euthanasia. The sweet death and transfiguration of that subject occurred toward the end of the eighteenth century.

The subjectivity of the transcendental Kantian subject is of a strictly logical nature. It is identified with the cognitive function. To know the possibility of all knowledge is the fundamental theoretical objective of the first Kantian *Critique*. The intention to understand what belongs to the human being, in this case the possibilities and the limits of the cognitive faculty, represents the turning point of philosophical rationality as *apodissi*.[111] Transcendental critical thought from Kant to Husserl adhered to this conception of philosophy as rational certainty. To understand the human is to know the person as pure subject of knowledge. Subjectivity consists of those "elements of knowledge that are discovered *a priori* within us."[112] Such elements are also revealed in those purely ideal and necessary original conditions, which are not determined by empirical and contingent contents.

Scheler's itinerary traces one of the most significant ways traversed by the thought running between the nineteenth and twentieth century. Scheler opposed the reduction of the subject to the pure ambit of logical operations. He also argued against subjectivity as logical structure rooted in the thought that constitutes consciousness of it. Gaos knows well that with Scheler the problem of the reform of the transcendental subject begins with the attempt to recover the affective or the emotional, in the territory of philosophical rationality taken as *apodissi*. Scheler applied the doctrine of the objective intentionality of knowledge, together with the Husserlian theory of eidetic intuition, to the sphere of emotional life. He intended to give an autonomous gnoseological foundation to ethics and to philosophy of religion.

Gaos proposed a possible definition of the affective.[113] The affective is not a form of knowledge, nor is it a content that can be learned empirically by cognitive operations. The affective, as being from the soul, cannot be intuited in space, or even in time, for it differs from states of the soul, understood as representations of the external senses. The affective, like every feeling of pleasure and pain, and will, remains excluded from our knowledge.[114] As Aldo Masullo, a thinker who has reflected at length on these subjects, put it: the affective is pure and simple fact. The logical can be thought in the purity of its ideality, independently of the factual. The affective or the pathic is pure factuality. If we remove the being of the affective as fact, nothing remains.[115]

Scheler has characterized the sphere of affectivity further as passive or receptive. He opposed the Kantian primacy of the activity of the transcendental "I." The orderer of the world-picture, the "I" stands opposed (*Gegen-stand*), as hostile object or "enemy" to dominate. Scheler has proposed the primacy of spiritual passivity. This attitude no longer of hate, but of love for the world, is an attitude of availability. We can grasp how those affective significates are given *a priori* in an experience, without any mediation. In short, Scheler's attempt to widen the field of the *a priori* to emotional experiences (either emotive states or affections) amplifies the sphere of subjectivity from purely logical ambit to the territory of emotive life.

The thought running between the nineteenth and twentieth centuries has been traversed in another way. The notion of the subject has been redefined by including subjectivity in ambits that are not purely logical-transcendental. This way, starting from Kantian philosophy, leads from Wilhelm Dilthey to Heinrich Rickert, up until the early Heidegger. Its conclusion in some respects is opposed to Kantian thought. Already in the latter half of the nineteenth century, Dilthey reassumed the Kantian project to establish the logical-epistemological constitution of historical sciences. He proposed a critique of historical reason and a reform of the transcendental subject. In opposition to the pure subject, cognitive, disembodied and abstract, to the "I think," Dilthey describes a willing, thinking, and sentient subject, the entire human being in its historical and social determination.[116] When redesigning, not just amplifying, the critical and transcendental problematic nature of Kantian philosophy, Dilthey observes: "We ought to leave the pure and refined air of the critique of Kantian reason, in order to satisfy the entirely different nature of historical objects."[117] In some passages of his *Breslauer Ausarbeitung*, he states:

> The *a priori* of Kant is rigid and dead; but the real conditions of consciousness and its presuppositions, such as I understand them, are a living, historical process. They are development. They have their history, and the course of this history is their adaptation to the multiple contents of the perception that is being recognized, more and more exactly, in an inductive fashion. History's life captures even the apparently rigid and dead conditions of our thinking.[118]

The interesting interlacing of themes that link Heinrich Rickert to Dilthey occur within the sphere of reflection that favors the real historicity of life. These thinkers differ on the distinction between sciences of nature and sciences of the spirit and on the field of gnoseology. In my judgment, as well as Rickert's, the fundamental cognitive problem is not one of pure knowledge, but of historical knowledge. The enlargement of gnoseology within the sphere of understanding what is human, permits reform of the transcendental subject. Consciousness in general (*Bewusstsein überhaupt*), universal and impersonal consciousness, to which every individual consciousness refers in formulating a valid judgment, is logical, ethical, and aesthetic consciousness. Once we abolish the antinomy between the theoretical and the practical spheres, we can understand a new subject, now no longer pure and logical, but a living historical subject.

The horizons acquired in the field of subjectivity with critical and transcendental matrix, the emotional horizon, as well as the real historicity of life, are key to the theme of subjectivity in twentieth-century thought. Martin Heidegger perceives in the affective or pathic an essential characteristic of human existence in the world. While expanding Dilthey's perspectives[119] and also going beyond them, Heidegger develops the theme of the historical Being-there from the ontological and existential point of view. I am not simply putting aside the diversity of theoretical positions between two thinkers, Dilthey and Heidegger. Instead, though aware of their differences, I intend to illuminate the continuity between their views.

For the Heidegger of *Sein und Zeit*, *a priori* knowledge of the affective is possible to the extent that he has radically reformed the notions of transcendental, subject, and knowledge. In the *Kantbuch* of 1929, Heidegger insists on equivalency between the *cogito* and time. He attempts to eliminate the purity in the Kantian transcendental subject. Even the categorial modes, by means of which the "I" as temporal, living subject is related to the totality of beings, assume a dynamic aspect. Heidegger frequently affirms that time does not exist along side of the *cogito*, without ties with it. The *cogito* itself is time. Temporality is the modality that constitutes subjectivity. The categories have a temporal origin. In sum, what is characteristic of the subject is not the logical, that synthetic unity of apperception which must accompany all my representations.[120] Instead, once we depart from the existential analytic of Being-there, the characteristic property of the subject is existence as "thrownness" and "care," finding oneself "emotionally situated in one's own being." Whence the importance of the affective.

I have alluded to the radical reform of the notion of knowledge. It is no longer undersood as a theoretical operation, or as "perceptive and contemplative apprehension of a precise object." Knowledge is, instead, "understanding," which "in every case, pertains to *Dasein's* full disclosedness as being-in-the-world."[121] As a vital conduit, knowledge is the life that becomes involved in itself. The theme emerges of the affective as informative understanding, in which existence and its self-knowledge are co-related. Subjectivity is not something to understand; it is the life that understands itself. Subjectivity is already self-understanding. And so the primacy of the affective emerges. The "state of mind" (*Befindlichkeit*), or the "ontological disposition"[122] and the understanding (*Verstehen*), are modes co-originally constitutive of the "There." These modes of being are existentially fundamental modes in which the Being-there is its There. Taken together with the "disclosedness" (*Erschlossenheit*) in which the affective consists, such modes signify the primacy of the affective.

We know how "the fundamental and ontological interpretation of the principles of the emotions" proposed a re-examination of phenomena as affects and feelings. Heidegger immediately recognizes the new position given to the analysis of emotive life as a merit of the phenomenology of his day. Scheler has, indeed, "guided the problematic to a consideration of how acts which 'represent' and acts which 'take an interest' are interconnected in their foundations." Nevertheless, for the author of *Being and Time*, in the Schelerian analysis "the existential-ontological foundations of the phenomenon of the act in general are admittedly still obscure." To Scheler, it was not apparent how a phenomenon like the "ontological disposition" (1) discloses "the Dasein in its thrownness and its submission to that world, which is already disclosed with its own being," yet (2) is "the existential kind of Being, in which the Dasein constantly surrenders itself to the 'world' and lets the 'world' matter to it in such a way that somehow Dasein evades its very self." Phenomenological interpretation "must make it possibile for Dasein itself to disclose things primordially and must . . . let Dasein interpret itself."[123] The ontological and existential significate of the ontological disposition then emerges. For me, the dominant theme is the primacy of the affective.

The Heideggerian road, and still earlier the Schelerian one, may have succeeded in effectively penetrating the dark depths of existence. In understanding the human being, they may have recovered the affective in the proposal of philosophical rationality as *apodissi*. In this regard, I would agree with some investigations that have shown the impossibility of grasping and dividing the affective insofar as factuality (*fattualitá*) in its pure modes and in its empirical residue.[124] More than in the issues or losses incurred as much by Scherlerian as by Heideggerian reflection, I am chiefly interested in the horizons that the two thinkers disclosed within the early twentieth-century philosophical scene. I am also curious about the influence that they have exercised on Western culture, particularly on Gaos. From his study of Scheler and Heidegger, Gaos inherited, developed, and transformed the theme of the pure logical subject's reform, of its euthanasia and rebirth as pathic subject.

Up to this point I have discussed the new horizon of the *Lebenswelt*. Life is a continuous process which, from the first moment, is somehow understanding of itself. Knowledge is self-understanding, affectively or emotively. Subjectivity's involvement with the world is pathic. I now want to examine the special sense of Gaos's reform of the subject. What is the characteristic or distinctive feature of the subject? According to Gaos, we must grasp, within the subject itself, the complex intersection of three dimensions: (1) *mocionalidad*, (2) plurality, and (3) transcendentality. Among the three, the level of *mocionalidad* is of the greatest interest to us. *Mocionalidad* characterizes subjectivity, as the heart or the central point from which the other dimensions radiate. I have already indicated how *mocionalidad* may be understood as the complex of inclinations, of volitions, either of the volitional sphere, or of psychic activity in its kinetic constitution.

Having distinguished *sensaciones* from *emociones* and *mociones,* and *emociones* and *mociones* from *conceptos*, Gaos determined that only emotions and motions of the mind, as psychical phenomena, exist purely and simply *in* the subject. Sensations, however, exist *for* the subject, and concepts exist *in* the subject, only by virtue of the characteristics that they have in common with psychical phenomena. In sum, the sphere of the psychical originates in the *emociones* and *mociones*. Let us grant that the psyche is pure activity. The active mode *par excellence* is motion. We can then conclude that the "psyche is pure *mocionalidad*."

The kinetic constitution of psychical activity is composed of three mutually complementary dimensions: (1) the level of thought (either of concepts or of thought's activity); (2) the level of *emociones*; and (3) the level of *mociones*. As in Dilthey's thought, Gaos's subject, living in its concrete determinateness, is a subject in which the spheres of thinking, feeling, and willing interact.

Thought is constituted by the cross-fertilization of three characteristics: first, its composition is formed by concepts; second, the hierarchical ordering among the concepts extends from the apex of the transcendentals to the lowest of the individual concepts; third, the dimension of thought's activity or *mocionalidad* interacts with the first two characteristics.

As for the ambit of *emociones* and *mociones*, they are truly so many and of such complexity as to appear irreducible to elementary modes, such as pleasure and pain. Nevertheless, some of them—love and hate among the *emociones* and will among the *mociones*—stand out as crucial and radical, from the point of view of the psyche. Even more intriguing than the psychical matter that constitutes *mocionalidad* is the formal motion constitutive of psychical activity in general. This *movimiento* expresses the passage from dissatisfactions to satisfactions, and then on again to new dissatisfactions and satisfactions. Another matter is whether such movement may be common also to the entire animal kingdom or to living beings in general. But only the typically human satisfactions and dissatisfactions are characterized by being consciously conceived, respectively, as goods and evils. The essential movement of the psyche as pure *mocionalidad* then is a movement from evils to goods, or, in a strict sense, from evil to good. This movement is also from the real to the ideal. When we are dissatisfied, the dissatisfaction is the real and the satisfaction is the unreal or the ideal. The movement becomes definitively manifest, when it goes "from unhappiness to happiness, and also, from unhappiness or from infinite evil, nothingness, to happiness and the infinite good, the Divinity, the Ideal, in capital letters."[125]

This is a crucial point. A problematic knot in Gaosian commentary is the passage from infinite evil, or from nothingness, to infinite good. If we are faced with a teleological movement, we ask ourselves about its sense. Does it mean that everything is organized with an end in sight, that is, the infinite good? Does the explanation of every passage—from dissatisfaction to satisfaction, from evil to good, from real to ideal, from unhappiness to happiness, from nothingness to infinite good—propose the end toward which that passage is directed? But here the end is the form or the *raison d'être*, according to which everything is ordered thus as it is ordered. Or else the end is the *raison d'être* of the movement itself, human *mocionalidad*. In other words, what makes possible proceeding from dissatisfaction to satisfaction to the infinite good is not the conclusive moment of the process. The end considered abstractly is separated from the single moments and independent of the process as it unfolds. The process depends, instead, on the movement constitutive of the process that originates from the subjectivity of the subject. Thus a cardinal position of traditional metaphysics is turned on its head. Let us suppose with Gaos that "the eudaemonic proof of God's existence has for a premise the *emocional-mocional* constitution of the human being."[126] The first principle has then slipped from the supreme Being, that used to explain itself and all else, to the human being, as "the fact or ultimate phenomenon, which gives the *raison d'être* for all other beings, inclusive of God." That slippage was made possible by arguing from the new typology of subjectivity.

Clearly here a notion of transcendence also comes into play. This notion of transcendence excludes a principle that exists beyond every human experience. Let us grant that the human being is the only existent that transcends itself "in the *emocional* and *mocional* movement that drives the person to conceive the end of self-transcendence." To the human being then belong the *emociones* of love and hate, directed toward our own satisfactions and those of others. These emotions motivate some *mociones* of a special kind: the volitions of existence and inexistence of subjects of love and hate. The role of the *mociones*, that is, of impulses, instincts, and volitions, is especially relevant in the context of psychic activity in general. This means: the cardinal-point of the intersection of the three dimensions that constitute the psychical sphere, the levels of thought, of *emociones*, and of *mociones*, is represented by the *mociones*. The psyche as pure activity has its root in *moción* as action, alteration, and inclination of the mind. Only *moción* has its own kinetic constitution. Thought and *emociones*, instead, are active. They participate in the movement of the *mociones*, that is, of the *mocionalidad*. The relation between thoughts and *emociones*, and the relation between thoughts and *mociones* are relationships of causality: "thoughts and *emociones* are mobile effects of the mobile will."[127] Thus, will expresses "the very movement of showing up, of presence, and existence," of the human psyche.

Gaos considers the subject as eminently *mocional*, even more than *emocional*. Distinguished by a special *dynamis* of will, the Gaosian subject differs from the pure logical subject, which suggests reification of permanence, and the immobilization of the "I." Does the assertion that will is the cause of all emotions and thoughts contradict the belief, frequently expressed, that the special *emociones* of love and hate cause the volitions of existence and of inexistence? This question disturbs Gaos's whole train of thought. Nevertheless, he believes that he can resolve the antinomy. Gaos distinguishes between (1) will in general as the cause of *emocionalidad* in general and (2) the *emociones*, in particular of love and hate, as cause of the volitions, in particular of existence and inexistence. I will return to this question, which seems invalidated by its aporetic appearance.

Let us consider, instead, the intrinsic relationships among (1) *mociones* of will and (2) *mociones* of impulses, instincts, and so on. Is will the cause of impulses and instincts? Or *vice versa*, is will determined by the sphere of impulses and instincts? What is special to the human being and makes a person human, so it seems to Gaos, is that everything "from the 'inferno' of the impulses up to the 'heaven' of thought," is involved with "the form of that specific movement of the continuous-will: the specific movement of the continuous creation of the psyche itself."[128] Human nature shapes and reflects an imbalance between real evil and ideal good. Within this "onto-axiological imbalance," the human being perennially oscillates. He or she is always precariously posed between nothingness and infinite good.

We have entered the impervious regions of instincts and impulses. However, we have not exhausted the exploration of the vast and ragged territory of the *mocionalidad*. A central problem remains to be examined: the modality characteristic of the subject's activity or the active modes of subjectivity itself. We must discover with what modal transcendentals the subject conceives itself.

If the subject conceives every existent by means of the transcendentals, then the subject must conceive itself, too, by means of these universal predicaments.

For Gaos, the transcendentals may be reduced to the two cardinals of contingent or possible finite existence and infinite or necessary existence, as opposed to inexistence or nothingness. By means of such concepts we conceive antinomically. Each existent can be conceived as finite or contingent (with the exception of the infinite and necessary cause of everything: theism); or as infinite or necessary (insofar as the substance of the existent is infinite and necessary: pantheism). Suppose that instead we consider as finite or contingent not only each existent, but rather all existence. We are then in the position characteristic of absolute contingency. Beyond possible combinations that can be realized, I must emphasize that conception itself is essentially antinomic. To emphasize the centrality of the problem of the antinomies does not mean to assert simply finitism as opposed to infinitism, or *vice versa*. It means to draw attention to the antinomic essence of the human being. The *emocional* and *mocional* antinomy is "the will of existence out of love for the existents, which stirs the desire for their infinite good, and the will of inexistence, out of hatred for the existents, which stirs the desire for their inexistence." This antinomy is the ultimate anthropological reality. Drawing attention to the centrality of this thematic idiom is useful for reconsidering the modal self-conception of the subject. The human being makes other existents consignees of his or her love and hate. He or she loves also himself or herself. With the modal transcendentals humanity conceives love or hate toward self:

> [M]an not only loves himself . . . he normally hates his dissatisfactions, his evils, and when he recognizes himself as the cause of them, he hates his wickedness, he hates himself.[129]

But, then, what is the special modal transcendental characteristic of human existence? When faced with the antinomy between finitude and infinitude, between possibility and necessity, the being of humanity chooses the road of possibility as the most appropriate one. At least until the time Gaos delivered the lectures, published under the title of *El más allá* (The Beyond), he strongly maintained "that human existence, unlike the remaining phenomona, possesses the modality of possibility, even as phenomenon." Human existence should be conceived solely with this modal transcendental. During the middle period of his speculation, Gaos regarded possibility as the fundamental conduit through which human existence flows.

How did Gaos understand this modal transcendental? The modal transcendental is not a logical possible, distinct from a real possible, as what does not include contradiction. These kinds of possibility are reducible to the not-impossible and inferred from the necessary. Nor is the modal transcendental to be understood in the sense of real possibility, which is identified directly with the potential, with what is destined inevitably to be realized. Gaos has clearly rejected the concept of possible as the necessary. He confronts the thesis of the reduction of possibility to necessity, often expressed during the course of Western thought. According to the victorious argument of Diodorus Cronus, for instance, all that is possible is made real. What is not made real is not possibile. Consequently, whatever is, is by necessity. And contrary to Nicolai Hartmann's fundamental modal law, Gaos sustains a diverse and opposed concept of possibility.

> Necessity cannot spring from possibility, without contradiction. Necessity either is *ab initio*, or better, *sine initio*; otherwise, it is not that necessity which equals infinitude. Therefore, the possibility that leads to necessity would be such only in appearance; fundamentally, such possibility already would be a necessary series.[130]

To say that the Gaosian concept of the possible re-enters the articulated panorama that the philosophy of existence has shaped of this category is to elude once again the specific and the determinate. In existentialism, at times the impossibility of the possible has been asserted, from Søren Kierkegaard to Martin Heidegger, at times the necessity of the possible, from Louis Lavelle to Gabriel Marcel, at times the possibility of the possible, from Enzo Paci to Nicola Abbagnano. So, what direction has the modality of possibility taken? For Gaos, authentic possibility is the disjunctive and indefinite one of potentiality-for-being or of non-potentiality for being: "if it can, sooner or later, only be or only not be, being or non-being becomes necessary." Therefore,

> the possibility of human existence, of the movement of the real union of good and evil—co-finite together—toward the ideal of the pure good—infinite—would mean the potentiality for being or not being, and indefinitely this ideal . . . always.[131]

Gaos would not affirm: the necessity for being, the necessity for the realization of the ideal (even in a transcendent dimension), the necessity for not-being, or the necessity for the annihilation of the ideal in the sphere of the world beyond. Thus, the certainty of immortality would be as precluded as the certainty of annihilation with death, as the certainty of God's existence, and as the certainty of God's inexistence.

This was, I repeat, Gaos's position at least up until the period of his collected lectures, *El más allá*. In the mature Gaos, especially in his *Del hombre*, a striking change of perspective occurs: "There does not exist any such phenomenality of finitude, contingency, or human possibility. Every finitude, contingency, or possibility is a mere manner of conceiving phenomena of appearance and disappearance; and, conceiving correlatively, in a transcendental and metaphysical mode, the infinitude that is necessity."[132]

Gaos's reconsideration of the modality of possibility is in terms of the structure and antinomic essence of the *mocionalidad*. We have frequently observed how the *mocionalidad* oscillates between will of existence out of love for existents and will of inexistence out of hatred toward them. Now conceiving the modality of the finite or the possible, conceiving the phenomena of appearance and disappearance, and, correlatively, on the transcendental level, infinitude or necessity, is equivalent to the "same conception of the phenomena of human *mocionalidad* as movement from good and evil combined toward the purity of the good, and antinomic conception of them: at times, as indefinite possibility; at times, as apparent possibility, leading to a necessity and unique reality."[133]

Thus, we no longer have only the disjunctive and indefinite possibility of the potentiality-for-being and the non-potentiality-for-being. We also have an apparent possibility, leading to necessity. The antinomic co-presence of this double modality of possibility, disjunctive possibility and the possibility reducible to necessity, challenged the eudaemonic proof for God's existence. As movement toward infinite happiness in the infinite essence, human existence would be proof for the existence of this infinite essence, if and only if the movement be necessary. But the necessity of such movement has been invalidated by Scholastic critics of the proof on the grounds that what is potential need not be actualized.

In summarizing and synthesizing the new conception of possibility outlined in *Del hombre*, I can quote Gaos's own words:

> [T]he conception prior to the modification was one of the possibility of the phenomenality of the human being: the modified conception is an antonimic one of human phenomenon as either possibility or necessity.[134]

But the conflict between possibility and necessity, and thus the co-presence of apparent possibility alongside of authentic possibility of the potentiality-for-being and the non-potentiality-for-being lead to a skeptical muddle. Gaos denied that possibility could be reduced to necessity, from the moment that necessity "either is *ab initio*, or better, *sine initio*, or it is not necessity."

In order to understand how the human phenomenon is at times possible, at times necessary, we must return to the omnipresent theme of the antinomies. We must refer to the antinomic essence, to the dual constitution of the human being. But, then, aren't authentic existential possibilities compromised in some way? And, on the moral level, don't we always face the antinomy between freedom and determinism? Let us grant that *mocionalidad* expresses the passage from dissatisfaction to satisfaction, from the real to the ideal, from evil or from nothingness to infinite good. *Mocional* disposition must be realized through human conscious self-determination. In this conscious self-determination, then, the human being is bound to fail the test of liberty.

Within a picture of references so wide and so rich with disquieting questions, I wish to sketch an important argument. The thematic idiom under discussion is the relation between existence and temporality, or the temporal condition that constitutes existence. Time is required for the modalization of existence through the modal transcendentals of finitude and infinitude. While finite existence can only be thought of temporally, infinite existence "on account of being a negative relation with time, does not permit a relationship with it." Existence, however, does not have relation with time, but is relation with it. In the same way,

> the modalities of possibility and necessity are in an essential relationship with time, even if only insofar as they are identified respectively with finite and infinite existence.[135]

Thus, a disjunctive duality that includes time is essential to possibility. The possibility of being or not being implies at least two successive moments: the first moment for the duality and the second for the realization of one of the terms of the disjunctive dyad. *Vice versa*, necessity, essentially united to the notion of eternity as timelessness, must exclude succession and time.

In this context, I do not propose to examine, thematically, a problem of such vast proportions as the conjugation of the cardinal transcendentals with the temporal element. Yet, I cannot remain silent about the interrogatives that this knot of questions carries with it. These queries begin with the meanings attributed to the notion of time, apart from its traditional meaning as motion or becoming. Let us grant that existence is relationship with time. Does that mean that time has an ontologically relevant significate? Is time the structure of the presence that characterizes existence? Perhaps time can be understood in other senses. Gaos's entire commentary appeared to revolve around a fulcrum: the pathic or *mocional* subject. Then can time, also, be understood as our suffering becoming? Is this the lived sense of becoming? In my chapter devoted to the phenomenology of the categories and to the theme of existence, I have discussed the relationship between presence and time and between phenomenon and time. Now I ask again about the lived sense of temporality. Yet, regarding this thematic idiom, insufficiently discussed by Gaos at least in *Del hombre*, many areas in his commentary remain in shadow. Awaiting capture, above all, is the distance between temporal existence, finite or possible, and timeless existence, infinite or necessary.

When drawing out the threads of the present commentary, let us remember that the plurality and transcendentality of the subject interact with the *mocionalidad*. I will refer briefly to these dimensions, for this topic is connected with the thematic idiom of *mocional* activity. On that account, rather than following in detail the course traversed by Gaos in his treatment of the new themes, I will summarize only his conclusions.

The plurality of subjects or of intersubjectivity cannot be disjoined from the fundamental characteristic of plurality itself. The historicity of plurality is manifested "in the fact that everything human has a history or a historical being, and everything means all things human, the human being inclusive, although all things human do not all have the same kind of historicity."[136] If everything human is historical, will the characteristics of *mocionalidad* and *modalidad* also be historical? And what is the role of historicity in the Gaosian vision? Can we consider Gaos an historicist thinker? One of the most radical expressions of contemporary historicism is Ortega y Gasset's thesis that "the human being does not have nature or essence, but rather has history." According to Gaos, Ortega's position is extreme, absolute, and disputable like "the absolute change of Heracliteanism confronted in the *Theaetetus*, and for the same reasons." Gaos asks himself if the extreme manifestations of historicist thought are not invalidated by a paradox. This paradox consists in the wish to substitute a new essence for the essences, from the moment that the concept of historicity was a concept of essence. This means recognizing that the human individual is not interchangeable, substitutable, reducible. Wishing to conjoin nature with history, universal with individual, we should proceed from a position of mediation that grants "a mode of the plurality of the human subjects and nothing more" ("un modo de la pluralidad de los sujetos humanos y no más"[137]) to historicity.

To further discuss this thematic idiom would be interesting. For the idiom adds to *mocionalidad*—beyond the single subject—the historical plurality of subjects, that is, historical self-consciousness. I am pressed, however, to treat the transcendental dimension of the subject.

An ideal phenomenological journey of subjectivity has been synthetically traced. It starts from an auroral consciousness of humanity as subject. The human being is at first represented as object, as thing among things. Humanity stands at the dawn of the long and arduous journey that leads from the cosmological philosophies to those that assume the priority of consciousness and to the idealist philosophies. A fundamental stage of this journey is marked by the consciousness of being subject-of-one's-own objects. Such consciousness oscillates between conceiving the subject as individual subject of one's own objects, *à la* George Berkeley, and as transcendental subject of those objects, "in the manner of the neo-Kantian interpretation of Kant and Fichte." The concluding stage at the conception of the transcendental subject requires that three essential conditions be met:

> [1] absolute identity or the absolute uniqueness of the "I"; [2] the total constitution of objects thanks to the concepts; [3] the unification of all concepts thanks to the "I."[138]

We are again at the point of our departure, the transcendental subject. A long and troubled journey was required in thought. The idea of the "I" as subject, in which thoughts inhere as its predicates, was replaced by the conception of the "I" as apperceptive consciousness. Such consciousness is synthetic activity, which, in judgments, determines the union of subject with predicate. But the transcendental subject, so constituted, has been placed in crisis, in a state of agony and death.

The crisis has risen from the very heart of the transcendental conceptions of the "I." It has evolved from the thought that goes from neo-Kantianism to Scheler, to Heidegger, and beyond. This journey leads to Gaos's reform of subjectivity and to his conception of the transcendental as work of the ethical antinomic constitution, *emocional* and *mocional*, of humanity. It is useful, in this regard, to allow Gaos to speak for himself:

> [T]he object of philosophical anthropology is the essence of humanity. This essence is reason, which is eminently the transcendentals. By means of the transcendentals, the rational subject conceives the existent, even itself, in an antinomic form. The transcendentals are work of the subject's *emocionalidad antinómica*. The antinomic nature of the transcendentals is work of the antinomy of the *emocionalidad*. The human being is an animal of dissatisfactions and satisfactions, and of a love or hatred for them, which motivate the will of infinitude or inexistence. This implies conceiving these feelings with the transcendentals of pure reason and the general terms of practical reason. Then, precisely to the extent that the human being is moral animal, the human being is the rational animal. . . .[139]

I have emphasized how the genesis of the antinomic nature of the principal categories of pure reason is linked, for Gaos, to the dual ethical constitution of the human being. Gaos wanted to provide a radical and subjective *raison d'être* for philosophy. What are the major differences between Gaos and that existential thought, which continually inspired him?

The focal point of Gaos's relation with Heidegger is relevant here. For Heidegger, the *primum* is the constitutive finiteness of the Being-there. Finiteness pertains to the way being presents itself. Isn't the problem of finite being the key to the foundation of metaphysics? From this condition of finiteness, which has nothingness before it—from which, however, *omne ens qua ens fit* (every being comes into existence insofar as it is a being)—we will embark upon the fundamental pathways of philosophical interrogation. In other words, the *primum* in play is the non-ontical constitution of the human being. Heidegger's commentary about moral conscience does not represent the Archimedian point for determining every other question.

For Gaos, the moral constitution of the human being is the origin of the categories of non-being and of their correlative onto-theological categories. Gaos affirms that Heidegger's work has had a decisive influence on his resolve to unravel "in due fashion, an exhaustive, systematic phenomenology of negation." But Gaos's radical difference from Heidegger, the author of *Sein und Zeit*, begins with the primacy that Gaos assigned to the dual ethical constitution of the human being and to the sphere of *mocionalidad*. Gaos observes that he disagrees with Heidegger on the fundamental point of his work. Heidegger, Gaos adds, believes that

> the non-ontical constitution of humanity is the origin of moral consciousness, which is limited to lend its quiet and anguished voice to such constitution, instead of thinking that the moral constitution of the human being is the origin of the categories of non-being, and of their ontic-theological correlatives. On this fundamental point, my course is pre-existentialist, unfashionable, not in the fashion of existentialism, itself already a bit out of fashion. Nor did I agree with the Heidegger, who, in his lecture on metaphysics, states that nothingness, which is present in itself, is the ontological nothingness of annihilation (*aniquilación*), and not the axiological nothingness of utter nullification (*anonadamiento*), and that this nothingness is the origin of negation; instead of thinking that the ethical-axiological constitution of the human being is the origin of negation and of the categories of non-being, and among these, the category of nothingness.[140]

But passing beyond Heidegger, Gaos holds that among the special virtues of his own commentary is that:

> he proceeded from the technical knowledge of the phenomenologists to the pathos and drammatic art of the Nietzscheans. He [Gaos] was re-Nietzschean as much as re-Kantian: the explanation of philosophy by means of subjectivity, that in Kant, resides in the spectral, transcendental subject of pure and practical reason, in Nietzsche, descends to the depths of the human, all too human subject, not fathomed even by the existentialists of subsequent generations, who no matter how dynamically they may have done it, have converted those depths into superficialities again by formalizing them.[141]

I have extensively quoted Gaos's words, because they allow us to glimpse the path (*Leitfaden*) that guides us along his speculative itinerary. Gaos's long journey into the depths of the human subject began with his denial of the transcendental subject. He reached as far as the boundaries of the affective. But has Gaos's conception of the "mocional" subject solved the problem of the transcendental subject? In other words, has the Gaosian way succeeded in penetrating the dark depths of existence? Or was it instead doomed to failure?

Gaos conjugated the sphere of *mocionalidad* with that of transcendental knowability. He reduced the hermeneutics of the entire ambit of emotions, impulses, volitions yet again to a transcendental type of schema. As much from Scheler's as from Heidegger's perspective, to grasp or to divide the affective (1) in its pure modes, knowable transcendentally, and (2) in its empirical residue, is impossible. Has Gaos finally found the royal road for exploring the abysmal profundities of existence?

Six

THE PROBLEM OF TIME

1. "Time," according to *Dos exclusivas del hombre: La mano y el tiempo*

So far we have frequented the fundamental routes of Gaos's speculation. Now we travel again through only one of the paths he explored. This path is an important crossroad of theoretical questions and problems. We are referring to the problem of time.

On various occasions, we have considered the centrality of this problem within the context of Gaosian theory. For Gaos, existence is essentially temporal activity. Temporality is the condition that makes the phenomenal activity of consciousness possible. Gaos articulates the problematic nature of what we are discussing here in a complex manner. He especially considers phenomenological time within the horizon of the possibility of an intentionally immanent consciousness. Yet, starting off from the unity of consciousness, which, in an intentional mode, encompasses the temporal ectases (*ek-stasi*) of the past, the present, and the future, we cannot again review the entire conjugation of psychic and physical phenomena with time. Nor can we again pose the questions that concern the waste matter between temporal finite existence and non-temporal infinite existence.

This round, our reference point is a work of 1944 entitled *Dos exclusivas del hombre: La mano y el tiempo*,[142] which comprises the text of the five lectures that Gaos delivered at the University of Nuevo León. In these essays, Gaos questions the distinctive traits of the human being, as compared with every other entity. These traits and characteristics seem to be represented symptomatically only by the hand and by time. While the body is the most distinctive (*más patente*), feature, the most radical feature is human time. Human time distinguishes the human being from all other timeless beings or *entes* and also from every other finite entity.[143] Let us leave out of consideration the first three lectures devoted to the hand. I will put aside Gaos's discussion of the caress (*caricia*) as the human act that expresses the language of the most intimate inwardness. The last part of the volume traces the general lines of the problem of time, starting from a phenomenology of temporality.

During a preliminary approach to the phenomenon of temporality, Gaos distinguishes the three modalities that characterize the temporal. A first mode is one of beings that appear deep within becoming. Such beings include minerals, plants, animals, and also the human being insofar as humanity, too, belongs to the animal kingdom: "Whatever comes into being, is and ceases to be in time, or is in time with beginning and end, is temporal in a primary and most appropriate sense."[144] A second temporal modality is characteristic of those beings such as souls and immortal spirits that have a beginning but no ending. Finally, the modality of beings such as God and purely ideal objects seems to escape time.

Nevertheless the modality of such beings without beginning and ending still belongs to the horizon of temporality. Indeed, "according to this primary meaning, the eternal itself is temporal, and in effect, the primary and popular representation of eternity is the one of time taken in its infinite totality."[145] To the temporal, in the third sense of the term, is opposed timelessness, that literally is "that which has nothing to do with time." Just as geometric figures have nothing in common with morality, and feelings nothing in common with volume, the same may be said of the relationship between timelessness and time: it is like asking, "What color is the sound of the flute?" or "Is morality spherical or cubical?"

After these introductory observations, Gaos reaches the heart of the problem by distinguishing two modes of the human relationship with time: one consists in being in time by being born, living, and dying. This mode is to suffer time, to allow oneself a passive life. The other mode consists not only in existing in time, but in "*living time* and the relationships of beings and things with time, including its characteristic relationships or the absence of such relationships" ("*vivir el tiempo* y las relaciones de los seres y las cosas con él, incluyendo las propias, o la falta de tales relaciones").[146] While the first mode joins the human being with inanimate beings, as well as with plants and animals, the second joins human beings with immortal souls. This relationship holds a special interest for the philosopher because it consecrates the appearance of consciousness or human liberty. But mankind has a long road to travel before reaching self-consciousness and acquiring the consciousness not of merely suffering time but of taking it up into the self. This is the phenomenological journey of the consciousness of time, which Gaos only schematically outlines. From "living in time," the first step of this journey, humanity passes to a type of knowing that calculates time in terms of chronology and chronometry. The human being then fashions "a commonplace representation of time itself, either as time of things, that is, as time concrete along with them, or as abstract time, time in general and unto itself."[147] Ultimately, humankind reaches the apex of the knowledge about time, the philosophy of time.

Gaos's principal problem is to capture, right from the start, the fundamental traits of the representation of time. He observes that a spatializing vision of time presents itself to us: "we represent time to ourselves as an entity distinct from those things that are temporal in every sense of the term, in other words, as an entity in itself." Or we represent time as something in which temporal things are arranged, like a container or an envelope. But, because time is distinct from what is contained in it, we represent it as empty and therefore homogeneous. Yet the moments or the instants that make up time, however absolutely homogeneous as they may be among themselves, are affected by a multiple heterogeneity. In the representation of time, the focal point is the only fully real dimension, the present, around which the dimensions of the past and the future crowd together. "Past and future moments are not real or they are not: the past because now they are no longer, the future because they are not yet."[148]

Let us set aside the problem whether his emphasis on the reality of the present and the consequent questioning of the *realitas* of the past and the future would place Gaos's reflections within the horizon of that current in Western thought which, from Augustine to Bergson, has expressed the idea of time as "intuited motion." Here a *vexata quaestio*, often proposed in the history of philosophy, is in play: the question whether time slips into nothingness, from the moment that the past exists no longer. Yet at every instant the present disperses into the past, and the future still does not exist. In what sense, then, can we speak properly of the reality of the present if it appears as the threshold (*limen*) between what is-not-yet and what is-no-longer? Wouldn't the consequence of all this be the questioning of the reality of the present? Apparently, Gaos became fully aware of such problems. He tried to obviate the difficulties by distinguishing between moments and instants. The characteristic of instants is to be point-shaped, lacking extension. Moments are endowed with some extension. They are susceptible to increase or decrease from an indivisible point to an ever greater extension. Gaos devotes special attention to moments, as time's general representation.

We can represent future moments, for example, forthcoming dates, which some day will begin to be past. In such a case, we do not imagine simply things or facts corresponding to dates. We imagine the dates themselves that are the moments of time. If, besides, we make the moments of the past present, we can view the total course of our lives from birth to death, and even the total development of universal history. But we can also imagine the present according to two distinct modalities: either (1) we calculate beforehand the change in the present, which "avanza a ser futuro y echa a sus espaldas momentos pasados" (moves on to become future, casting past moments behind itself),[149] or (2) we notice the present that passes into the past, that "pasa a ser pasado" (passes to be past), as it happens when we feel the fugitive quality of all things and of our lives. Here our representation of time is a flux, a course, a movement, and a change. What prevails, in short, is the idea of an "estructura *cinética*, dinámica" (*kinetic*, dynamic structure). But is it possible to imagine it so, without having the image of a motionless network of time? Does an extended texture exist within time's "substrate," situated below the dynamic design? Whether time is single or twofold, in motion or static, we represent it in general (if I may continue with the spatial metaphor) as one-dimensional, longitudinal or linear, rectilinear, and, in addition, as infinite, without beginning or end, marching toward an unlimited future. Further, when we represent time in itself, as distinct from things, we make it present[150] to ourselves generally as a movement of uniform velocity. However, in some cases phenomena seem to impart their velocity, fast or slow, to time. Time then appears to quicken or to slow down.

We must therefore proceed to the representation of things deep within time. We need to ask about the meaning of the preposition "in" in the expression "to be in time" (*ser en el tiempo*) with or without beginning and end. In the first place, we have the meaning of a spatial, material inmost being. But such an inmost being presents a double incoherence: it is one-dimensional and in a sense, infinite; yet, it is also a spatial if not material inmost being, which is ill-reconciled with a characteristically temporal horizon, for which the topical dimension proves inadequate.

We may, instead, abandon the representation of things in time in order to represent a relationship of things with time. Doesn't this *a priori* time—which gives order to phenomena and disciplines their succession—doesn't this time, understood as a "container," in which beings find their collocation, end up being itself atemporal? It lies beyond that motion which it ought to explain. Is time the horizon for putting the question about the modality of being's manifestation? Let us suppose that the question "What is a thing?" exists at the center of philosophical interrogation. The problem of how a thing is, of its self-disclosure beyond its endurance and its disappearance, also occurs. The question of characterizing time as the dynamic structure that permits being to be encountered then arises. Temporality presents itself as the horizon within which the mode of phenomenal self-disclosure is recorded. We commonly observe that things move and pass away in time. Time, in turn, produces and annihilates things. Yet timelessness, instead, is represented as never destined to pass away, as *perduradero* (enduring) or *perdurable* (everlasting), incapable of change, within an eternal present.

For Gaos, we represent time as a *movimiento sin móvil*, an absolutely pure movement. But is such a movement representable without representing things in the act of moving, however abstract those entities may be?[151] The moments of time are the mobiles and time is the motion of these mobiles. In reality, our inadequate representation is due to the fact that our notion of time is an abstraction entirely forced out of concrete time, from the motions of the mobiles. The distinctness of time in relation to things and its empty homogeneity are the completed expression of this abstraction, more imaginative than conceptual, and, therefore, imprecise and imperfect. I insist that we would be in error to conceive time as a container that contains all other things: better to conceive it as an extremely careful abstraction.

Nevertheless, only concrete time is real: the other is nothing but our artificial elaboration. We should, therefore, turn the initial representation upside down: "instead of things being in time, it is time that is in things, in finite things, their finite motion."[152] Each of the mobiles has its own motion, different from that of the others. And mobile or temporal beings are distinguished from immovable or timeless ones precisely because of such motion, which is temporality.

But if only concrete time is real, how do we arrive at the key to the problem? How do we respond to the question "What is time?" Our answer will not come from theory of knowledge, from understanding, for example, time as an "*a priori* form of sensibility." Neither science nor philosophy, according to

Gaos, is capable of affirming the talisman or the passkey to the question. In his judgment, the royal road of time's problem exists in the careful, meticulous analysis of current expressions that we encounter in everyday language: "to have time," "to gain or lose time," "to pass the time," "to kill time." These expressions connote a relationship between the human being and time, a relationship not given between any other being and time.[153]

These expressions can be applied only to a human being. About no other entity, be it a rock, a plant, an animal, or even the immortal beings, angels and God, can we say that it loses or gains time.

> The existence of such expressions signifies that common, pre-philosophical wisdom already knows something about the relationship between the human being and time: philosophy must potentiate ("potenciar") this common, pre-philosophical knowledge. . . . What is, then, the common significate—ultimate, radical, philosophical—of such expressions? To what common, radical phenomena or reality do they refer?[154]

Let us put aside further Gaosian speculation on time, which leads to reflection on the human being's finite being and, from there, to the theme of death.[155] We shall pose, instead, a radical question, the final question which is posed by Gaos himself: What is the ultimate significate of the common expressions about time? Is philosophy's task one of potentiating common, pre-philosophical knowledge?

The limit reached by Gaos is the last threshold of questioning. It indicates yet again the block reached by predicative thought when it inquires about time: not philosophy but the expressions of everyday language say something about time. This, in a nutshell, is the Gaosian thesis.

2. The Aspects of Time within Western Tradition

So far we have followed Gaos during his reflections. Now let us recall the most general coordinates of the problem. I will summarize the most significant moments, the diverse kernels, the essential problematic knots of the unique polyhedral question about time. My intention is not to propose a historiographical synthesis of the argument. I want to rethink the Gaosian thematic idiom within a theoretical context that will serve as a background. This ideal stage will establish a point of comparison with Gaos's special arguments.

We may distinguish three fundamental conceptions of time during the course of Western thought. The first, elaborated since antiquity, has understood time essentially as the measurable order of motion. This conception represents the common denominator among ancient philosophers. We may think of the renowned Aristotelian doctrine of time as "number of motion in respect of 'before' and 'after'";[156] of the Stoics' thesis according to which time is "the interval of the cosmic motion"; and the Epicurean definition of time as "a property" or "an accompaniment of motion." Well known, also, is how successful such an ordering of ideas was throughout the Middle Ages: realists, such as Albertus Magnus and Thomas Aquinas, and nominalists, such as William of Ockham, again proposed the Aristotelian canonical definition. Despite the critiques leveled at this definition during the Renaissance, even Descartes, well into the seventeenth century, repeated the definition of time as "measure of movement."[157]

In the modern age, this ancient conception rises again from the foundation of the Newtonian theory of mechanics. The uniformity of motion that is assumed as measure of time corresponds to the uniform flow of absolute duration. Often critical literature has confirmed the problematic nature of Kant's position on time, present in his fundamental work the *Critique of Pure Reason*, which still accepts the principles of Newtonian physics. Certainly more than in the *Transcendental Aesthetic*, the true Kantian treatment of time develops in the *Transcendental Analytic*. The second analogy of experience is labeled "Principle of Succession in Time, in accordance with the Law of Causality."[158] From the moment a thing attains its determined place in time, the order of succession is the causal order, provided that the order of successive perceptions is necessary. The objective succession consists in "that order of the manifold of appearance, according to which, in conformity with a rule, the apprehension of that which happens follows upon the apprehension of that which precedes."[159] The temporal series cannot be reversed, because "once the preceding state is in place, the event necessarily and invariably follows." Therefore, it is "the necessary law of our sensibility and formal condition of all our perceptions that the time preceding determines necessarily the time following." Unlike the imagination, which can reverse the order of events, the order of temporal succession is univocally a causal order. But here arise a series of problems and disquieting questions. The radical diversity between the imagination and the order of temporal succession has been discussed. But then is that really how things stand? Or does a more radical relationship link imagination to time? The reference of the categories of the understanding to time may take place in the *schemata* through the work of the pure imagination. The two trunks of our knowledge, sensibility and intellect, are unified by a common root, imagination. Besides, in the first edition of the *Critique of Pure Reason*, Kant himself confirmed the reciprocal implicatory relationship between imagination and time. Later he withdrew from the abyss that the analysis of imagination had opened. Kant surrendered to the traditional primacy of the *logos*. Nevertheless, the Kant of the second edition of the *Critique* is the philosopher who moves unequivocally to reduce time to the causal order.

Opposed to this principal conceptualization of time is a conception that signified the authentic watershed between the ancient world and the reflection of moderns. I am referring to Plotinus's thought and to Saint Augustine of Hippo. Time is the very life of the soul that extends toward the past or toward the future (*extensio* or *distensio animi*). For Augustine, past and future do not exist. The three ectases of time are thus improperly distinguished. We should say, instead, that three times exist in the soul: (1) the present of the past, which is memory; (2) the present of the present, which is direct intuition; and (3) the present of the future, which is expectation. This is the way Augustine puts it:

> It is in my own mind, then, that I measure time. . . . I say, that I measure time in my mind. For everything which happens leaves an impression on it, and this impression remains after the thing itself has ceased to be. It is the impression that I measure since it is still present, not the thing itself, which makes the impression as it passes and then moves into the past. When I measure time it is this impression that I measure. Either, then, this is what time is, or else I do not measure time at all.[160]

The idea of time as intuited motion or "intuited becoming," according to Hegelian expression, has traversed the whole of Western culture up to our day and age. Think of the Hegel of the *Encyclopedia*, of the Bergson of the *Essays* and of his theory of lived time, the idea of the duration of consciousness. Think of Husserl and the doctrine of "lived intentionality," as flux of consciousness, constitutive of time, where perception is a part of a "continuity of act," that is, memory and expectation.[161] The intentional movement of consciousness stretches out the present toward the past and toward the future. Consciousness orders the continuous retreat of primary memory into the past and its weakening to the point of vanishing.

Finally, twentieth-century existentialist thought reduces time to the structure of existence understood as possibility. In the history of Western metaphysics the dimension of the present has always been privileged. Now the primacy of the future is strongly noted. Time is, in origin, the future as coming toward (*zu-kunft*), as Heidegger has confirmed in a special way. Being-there is always open to itself, whether in an authentic or an inauthentic mode: "Dasein understands itself, and in such a way that this understanding does not merely get something in its grasp, but makes up the existentiell [*sic*] Being of its factical potentiality-for-Being."[162] In other words, the sense of the being of Being-there is the self-understanding of Being-there itself. Its original existential projection is to anticipate decision. The primary sense of existentiality occurs in the futural, which, however, does not signify

> a "now" which has *not yet* become "actual" and which sometime *will be* for the first time. We have in view the coming [*Kunst*] in which Dasein, in its ownmost potentiality-for-Being, comes towards itself. Anticipation makes Dasein *authentically* futural, and in such a way that the anticipation itself is possible only in so far as Dasein, *as being*, is always coming towards itself—that is to say, in so far as it is futural in its Being in general.[163]

Not by accident Heidegger insists that ecstatico-horizonal temporality becomes temporalized primarily by taking the future as its starting point. He intends to confirm the distance between his conception and the ordinary interpretation of time as a series of now-points or as an infinite succession of instants. Not that the "now" is pregnant with the "not-yet-now, but the Present arises from the future in the primordial ecstatical unity of the temporalizing of temporality."[164] In the Heideggerian hermeneutic ontology, even time must refer to the hermeneutic circle: whatever we envisage in the future as coming toward is what has been already, and *vice versa*. It is then quite a different discourse, which we need not develop here, whether the past is the dimension from which future possibilities depart, and whether the future is the possibility of changing or preserving the past. The future signifies, instead, the special prominence accorded to possibility, or to the conjugation of temporality with possibility. The horizon of time is the possible, and no longer the causal order.

But have we disclosed the essence of time and determined its own properties? Or, does time's innermost nature still escape Western speculation to the extent that it has never ceased to inquire about this disturbing problem? The numerous and often divergent attempts to understand the question conceptually demonstrate the difficulty in bringing to light time's hidden face. And then, with what expressions or with what categorial modes can we represent or tell time? In contemporary philosophy, the question is more alive than ever.

Some recent reflections on the theme appear certainly suggestive but not resolved. One thinker, Giacomo Marramao, intends to put the historiographical paradigm into crisis. Beginning with St. Augustine, this paradigm has permeated "the entire experience of the Western world in the modern era"; that is, "the oppositional scheme, antithetical to the linear one, of temporal authenticity (or interiority) and spatial inauthenticity (or exteriority)" within which the components of lived experience are assumed.[165] Marramao wishes to recover an aeonian idea of time, which appears in some paradigms in Western culture at its beginning, as in Plato, and in the oriental cosmological reflection of the Chinese canon of Mo-Tzu (fifth to third centuries B.C.). This aeonian idea consists of "an intuition and a message that are very ancient: the quintessence of time is one with its eternal spatial projection." In sum,

> Space is no longer considered as the death of Time, as the extinction of Time's fluid authenticity in the exclusive rigor of chronometric measurement; but spatialization seems as a *conditio sine qua non* for being able to experience, even at minimal and daily levels, how much happens to us.[166]

At this point, I would ask whether twentieth-century thought, at least beginning with "the second" Heidegger, has not already recovered the essential co-originating nature of both the spatial and temporal dimensions. Indeed, in *Being and Time*, Heidegger moves in the direction of understanding being as spatiality and free openness. And Hegel had already seen in time the *Aufhebung* of space, the element in which the multiplicity of experience is gathered within a punctuated consciousness.[167]

Putting aside, for the time being, the questions and suggestions that come from recent philosophical thought, I seek to draw out the threads of the present discourse. At this point, I could ask to what conceptual horizon we may refer Gaos's reflections on time. We could investigate the common traits between his belief in the nonexistence of the ectases of past and future and the conception of time as "intuited becoming." We could discern similarities between Gaos's view and the other two principal theorizations to which I have referred: the one that, since antiquity, has understood time as the measurable order of motion, or the other, which, more recently, has conceived it as the structure of existence.

The historiographical perspective is not what interests me. Granted that I have rapidly reconstructed the ragged archipelago that Western reflection on time has drawn during the course of its secular history. I have excluded fragments and minor islands, in my attempt to express clearly the great thematic lines that have constituted the principal entry ways to the problem of time. Yet I have sought to pursue, instead, a theoretical purpose: to place Gaos's speculation on time in the foreground of the problematic horizon of our theme. Beginning with a synthesis of the complex and articulate itinerary which Western thought has constructed about the theme of temporality, from the ancient Greeks up to ourselves, I have characterized the pathway drawn by Gaos. I want to characterize it in order to "repeat" the Gaosian problem, that is, to get to the root of his questions and of his way of putting them. For that reason, let us turn yet again to the essential problematic knots described by Gaos.

3. "Repeating" the Problem of Time with Gaos and beyond Gaos

We have considered how, in order to privilege the relation of things with time, Gaos has questioned the idea of *a priori* time that orders the succession of phenomena. *A priori* time is like an empty container where entities find their location. But perhaps the relationship of things with time is more radical. It is useful to ask about the being-thing of the thing, or about the correlation of the thing to being and to nothing. Suppose that with the ancient Greeks, a thing is what it is, but was not, and will change to not be. The reason is due to its relationship with being and nothing. For this reason, the ancient Greeks called the thing being (Latin *ens*), that which becomes. Perhaps this is the "place" where the infinite distance that separates being from nothing is gathered together. What then is the relationship of one thing with all other things? And what makes possible the leaving and returning of the thing into nothing? To ask about these problems means to radicalize the question: "Why therefore *ens*?" It is not immaterial if the sense of becoming is assigned to the totality—be it the Idea, God, or the Absolute Spirit—or whether there may be free play, freed from every

chain, a play where the becoming of beings unfolds according to an unpredict-
able, spontaneous creativity.

Gaos was confronted with such questions, even during the full maturity of
his thought. In *De la filosofía* and *Del hombre*, Gaos understood philosophy, first
of all, as *logon didonai*. Philosophy is to give a reason for the existence of the
existent and of the implicatory relation between the existent and the in-existent
or the non-existent. Gaos assumed that inexistence, along with the consequent
problem of the negative and negation, is an object of philosophy. Inexistence is
a more radical and more decisive object than existence itself. Gaos does not
seem to have attained the same problematic horizon in *Dos exclusivas del
hombre: La mano y el tiempo*, written some twenty years earlier.

To the question of the relation of things with time is linked another
important motif discussed by Gaos: the crisis of the model of one-dimensional,
longitudinal, or rectilinear temporality. The crisis of time is understood as an
infinite road, without beginning or end, in the direction of an unlimited future.
But here, too, a more radical question comes into play. Suppose that linear
temporality is in crisis. Should we then appeal to the idea of time as circle? And,
if not to circular time, to what else? Is it enough to question the linearity of time,
articulated in the three ectases, each irrepeatable, of present, past, and future,
without demanding the sense of every single moment. Need we choose between,
on the one hand, the idea of Judeo-Christian matrix, which represents time as
scanned by unique moments, not repeatable, such as the Creation, the Fall, the
Redemption, the Apocalypse, and, on the other hand, the Greek idea of circular
time, of the circular structure of becoming? Let us put aside linear temporality,
where every instant is a son that devours his father, only to be devoured, in turn,
by the next instant. Suppose we seek out the sense of every single moment. Must
we also mend (and in what way?) the caesura between that sense and the lived
event? This caesura has been noted many times during the course of Western
metaphysics. But grant that time is a circle. Must we then always return to stop
on the threshold of the gate on the boundary of the *eternal instant*? Here, as
Zarathustra has indicated, the path that leads to the gate from behind joins the
other path that leads onward from the gate. The two paths cross that continue for
an eternity. We would then succumb to the idea of the eternal return. And every
small and great thing in life would return an infinite number of times, every
thought and breath, and the very instant in which we affirm the return of every
thought and breath. Will this be the curse that makes us throw ourselves to the
ground, gnash our teeth, and curse the demon that has insinuated the worrying
doubt that we must live innumerable times, without anything new, the life that
we now live? Or perhaps this will be our happy destiny, our only salvation from
time's irredeemable fugitiveness, from its flowing into nothingness, from the
vanishing of being into non-being.

I could enunciate other problematic knots that are tied to the questions that
I have been discussing. But wishing to draw out the threads of the present

discussion, I am pressed to rethink the conclusive point of Gaos's inquiry on time. This point is the most original feature of his speculation: the royal road to the problem of temporality does not exist in predicative thought but in expressions of everyday language such as "to have time," "to gain or lose time," "to pass the time," "to kill time." Such expressions denote the human being's most singular relationship with time.

Having confirmed, however, the failure or impossibility of predicative thought to speak ineffable time, our question changes course. No longer "How is it possible to think time?" our question recognizes the impossibility of expressing time in accordance with the universality and the necessity of the categorial forms of knowing. Thinking with Gaos and beyond Gaos, let us suppose that temporality coincides with *ek-sistence*, that is, the self's continual self-differentiation. In addition, we grant that existence is the very fact of existing. Existence is not form or object of knowledge but factuality, from which nothing is left, once its being-as-fact has been removed. How then will we find the words that enable us to speak about time? A caesura occurs between the significate[168] and sense. What can be objectivized into logical forms or rationalized from the categorial point of view is separated from what can be expressed only by negation, which is how the non-logical can be thought. Suppose we abandon the kingdom of the significates in order to move into the pure sphere of sense. Will we be able only to feel time, that is, to suffer becoming? We feel pleasure and pain, the affects of the soul or the lived experiences, by which "animate" being is related to its own vital ambience. Will we only feel time without being able to communicate the experience of pleasure and pain and, therefore, also the experience of time? But if time is nothing other than the lived feeling of becoming, we can only repeat with Augustine that we know what time is, provided no one asks us what it is. We do not know what time is, if we must relate it to whomever inquires about it. In sum, the insurmountable difficulty of bringing to light time's countenance returns, however much like Augustine we confess that the drops of time (*stillae temporum*) are too precious for us and we are burning with the "desire to penetrate this most intricate enigma."

I come quickly to my conclusion. We have followed Gaos on a long and complex road. He has posed the philosophical question *par excellence*, "Why being rather than nothingness?"—sometimes as if in a low voice, sometimes shouting it with passion. Gaos has often reiterated it in the major works, *De la filosofía* and *Del hombre*, where he has linked this question with the problem of time. In these books, inquiring about being, Gaos does not discern the foundation of the universe in the "to be." The moral constitution of the human being is the origin of the me-ontological categories and of the onto-theological correlative categories. In *Dos exclusivas del hombre: La mano y el tiempo*, inquiring about time, Gaos has discerned the *Abgrund*, the abyss, the non-foundation: the defect of thought and language—of the *logos*, in short—when talking about time. We lack the language capable of speaking the names of being, of not being, or of the foundation. We also lack a language appropriate for expressing time, if we omit expressions of daily life.

We ask ourselves if other ways may exist of bringing to light time's countenance. What of the language entrusted to the power of the symbol, or to mystical experience, or to the allusiveness of the metaphor? And having cast off every intellectual arrogance, are we left with the possibility of listening in the silence? This silence is not dumb. It is the greatest amount of expressiveness of the word, or the manifestation of an expressive "beyond." Are we left listening to all the voices rising from the world scene, as the voice of the rivers, of the sea, and of the wind? The friendly voice of the wind that, passing among the leaves of the trees and making them rustle, can evoke in the poeticizing mind, the infinity of time, the eternity, where the human and natural seasons flow together and disperse up to "la presente e viva, e il suon di lei" (the current, live season, and the sound it makes).[169] And if reason ought to renounce its inquiry, predicative thought can say no more, but is able to affirm only what is not. What remains is the sweet abandoning of the intellect into the infinity of the time evoked by the sapient magic of the artist:

> And, listening to the wind rustle through this foliage, I am absorbed in comparing that infinite silence to this voice: and I conjure up the eternal, and the seasons that have died, and the current one, alive still, and its own sound. Thus, in this immensity, my thought drowns: and the shipwrecking is sweet to me in this vast sea.[170]

But we need to return and to reflect further on all of this.

NOTES

Editorial Foreword

1. Pio Colonnello, *Tra fenomenologia e filosofia dell'esistenza: Saggio su José Gaos* (Naples, Italy: Morano Editore, 1990). [Editor's note]

Author's Preface

2. Hans-Georg Gadamer, *Heideggers Wege: Studien zum Spatwerk* (Tübingen, Germany: Mohr, 1983). This work has been translated into English by John W. Stanley as *Heidegger's Ways: Hans-Georg Gadamer* (Albany: State University of New York Press, c. 1994). [Editor's note]

Chapter One

3. The elections of 12 April 1931, which resulted in the resounding victory of the leftist, reform parties and prompted the immediate departure of King Alfonso XIII, legitimized the installation of the Republic in Madrid. The violent, often bloody factionalism that for the next five years ensued with disastrous consequences in Spanish politics and social life, provided the military leaders with a custom-built cause, a self-appointed crusade, to rise on 17 July 1936 against the government. The stage was set for one of the most vicious conflicts in history: the Spanish Civil War, which lasted until March of 1939. Throughout the internecine conflagration, which, according to reliable estimates, claimed close to a million lives, the loyalists, better known simply as Republicans, clinging, with the glaring exception of the Basque contingent, to an anticlerical, socialist agenda, clashed with the "Nationalists," the forces of the political right, led by Generalissimo Francisco Franco y Bahamonde. For a full account of this troublesome period, see Gerald Brenan, *The Spanish Labyrinth: An Account of the Social and Political Background of the Civil War* (Cambridge, England: The Cambridge University Press, 1960), and Hugh Thomas, *The Spanish Civil War* (New York: Colophon-Harper, 1963). [Translator's note]

4. Homero Serís in 1945 and Ricardo Gullón in 1959 made use of the label "Generación de 1936" to designate a group of Spanish writers and intellectuals, born between 1906 and 1914, who came of age during the Civil War and were deeply affected by the dreadful event. Despite some reservations voiced by critics such as Guillermo de Torre, Serís's and Gullón's designation has achieved wide currency. It is now customary among historians of Spanish letters to employ the term loosely and to account for two generations, for whom the Civil War became a defining experience: the writers of 1927 and those of 1936. Cf. Ricardo Gullón, "The Generation of 1936," trans. Francis L. Trice; and Guillermo de Torre, "The Generation of 1936 . . . for the Second Time," trans. Daniel P. Testa and Carol Dana, in *Spanish Writers of 1936 (Crisis and Commitment in the Poetry of the Thirties and Forties): An Anthology of Literary Studies and Essays*, ed. Jaime Ferran and Daniel P. Testa (London: Tamesis, 1973), respectively, pp. 7-16, 17-21. [Translator's note]

5. On the basis of their respective attitudes toward exile, José Luis Abellán distributes these intellectuals into three groups: (1) those who lent their unconditioned support to the Republican cause and, realizing that the war had been lost, emigrated from Spain never to return to their homeland (for example, Antonio Machado, Joaquín Xirau, Eugenio Imaz, J. Serra Húnter, María Zambrano, and, last but not least, José Gaos); (2) those who could not, or would not, abandon their country and ended up spending the rest of their lives in jail (for example, Julián Besteiro, Professor of Logic in Madrid, who died in the penitentiary of Carmona, in the province of Seville); (3) those who became known as the exponents of "Third Spain," the likes of José Ortega y Gasset, Julián Marías, Xavier Zubiri, Gregorio Marañón, Ramón Pérez de Ayala, who mostly professed neutrality or showed indecision, refused to take part in the conflict, and went into exile at the outset of the Civil War. Abellán cautions us against a certain artificiality, or an excess of generalization, inherent in his scheme. A case in point is that of Manuel García Morente, who, after espousing the Republican cause, was persecuted by the "Reds" and forced to escape. After a few years in America, he returned to Spain, converted to Catholicism, and was ordained as a priest. He devoted the last phase of his career to teaching at the University of Madrid. (Cf. J. L. Abellán, *Panorama de la filosofía española actual: Una situación escandalosa* [Madrid: Espasa-Calpe, 1978], pp. 115-116.) A case apart, also, is that of Miguel de Unamuno. At the beginning, Don Miguel adhered to the "Alzamiento Nacional," as Franco's "Movement" was called, but then on 12 October 1936, during the opening ceremonies for the new academic year, he raised his voice defiantly to the face of a Franquista military official. On 22 October, Franco relieved Unamuno of his post as Rector of the University of Salamanca. From that day on, Unamuno lived, confined to his own house, in a voluntary exile until his death (31 December 1936).

6. Those who were students at that time lend their testimony as to the imposition of Scholasticism "as the only form of thought possible" in Spanish academic life. Carlos París, one such student, confesses that:

In some cases, a veritable frenzy of Scholastic orthodoxy occurred, identified with Thomism. In the halls of the various universities (this is one of my memories as a student) the frenzy went as far as to maintain that Suárez was a heretic because he had broken with Saint Thomas. (Cf. Carlos París, *El rapto de la cultura* [Barcelona: Laia, 1983], pp. 57-58.)

7. Within García Bacca's vast production, these titles deserve special mention: *Existencialismo* (Xalapa, Mexico: Universidad Veracruzana, 1962); "Existencialismo alemán y existencialismo francés: Heidegger y Sartre," *Cuadernos Americanos* (July-August 1947); "El sentido de la nada en la fundamentación de la metafísica según Heidegger, y el sentidode la nada como fundamentación de la experiencia mística según San Juan de la Cruz," *Cuadernos Americanos* (November-December 1944); *Antropología filosófica contemporánea* (Barcelona: Anthropos, 1982), particularly, "El plan de la antropología filosófica en Heidegger," ch. 9, pp. 159-172. Even though García Bacca is not an existentialist through and through, we should acknowledge that in his thought are some existentialist themes. Besides, he exhibits a keen historiographical sensitivity for the philosophy of existence.

8. We should mention, besides the philosophers already cited, Eduardo Nicol, who contributed to the general discussion on existentialism, without actually taking part in that movement. Nicol became a refugee in Mexico City, as soon as Franco came to power. See his *Historicismo y existencialismo. La temporalidad del ser y la razón* (Mexico: Fondo de Cultura Económica, 1950). Of particular interest is Nicol's controversy with Gaos, reflected in Gaos's retort in "De paso por el historicismo y el existencialismo," *Filosofía y Letras*, nos. 43-44 (1951). For a survey of the Spanish and Hispano-American philosophy of the twentieth century, see the bibliography appended to this monograph.

9. Published in Madrid, 1847. [Translator's note]

10. On Balmes see, among others, Ignasi Casanova, *Balmes. La seva vida, el seu temps, les seves obres* (Barcelona: Biblioteca Balmes, 1932); Juan Roig Gironella, *Balmes, filósofo: Investigación sobre el sentido íntimo y actualidad de su pensamiento* (Barcelona: Edit. Balmes, 1969); Alain Guy, *Les philosophes espagnols d'hier et d'aujourd'hui* (Toulouse: Privat, 1956), vol. 1, pp. 115-122; vol. 2, pp. 69-75.

11. "Criteriology" (*criteriologia*) is a branch of logic which presents a theory of means and methods, whereby thought distinguishes the true from the false. [Editor's note]

12. Edmund Husserl, *Ideen zu einer reinen Phänomenologie und phänome-nologischen Philosophie*, vol. 1, (Halle a. d. S.: M. Niemeyer, 1913). Translated by W. R. Boyce Gibson as *Ideas: General Introduction to Pure Phenomenology* (London: Allen and Unwin, 1931). [Translator's note]

13. Max Scheler, *Der Formalismus in der Ethik und die materiale Wertethik* (Formalism in Ethics and the Ethics of Material Values), 2 vols. (Halle a. d. S.: M. Niemeyer, 1913-1916). [Translator's note]

14. In the etymological components (*pan, en, theós*) of "panentheism," a term coined by Karl Krause, the neologism indicates a novel interpretation of the presence of the universe in God. A recent article on this subject is Armand F. Baker, "The God of Miguel de Unamuno," *Hispania*, 74 (1991), pp. 824-833, especially, p. 824. [Translator's note]

15. Karl Christian Friedrich Krause (1781-1832) established his reputation as a disciple of Johann Gottlieb Fichte and Karl Leonhard Reinhold. He followed in Kant's footsteps and became a rival of Georg Wilhelm Friedrich Hegel and Friedrich Wilhelm Schelling. Krause taught at Jena, Dresden, Berlin, Göttingen, and Mainz. For a list of Krause's works, see: *Entwurf des Systems der Philosophie* (1804), *System der Sittenlehre* (Leipzig: C. H. Reclam, 1810), *Das Urbild der Menschheit* (Dresden: Arnoldishchen Buchhandlung, 1811), *Vorlesungen über das System der Philosophie* (Göttingen: In Commission der Dieterich'schen Buchhandlung, 1828). Worthy of special mention are these studies on Spanish Krausism: Alain Guy, "Der spanische Krausismus als religiöse Grundhaltung," *Krause-Tagung* (Hofgeismer, Evangelische Akademie, 27-29 November 1981); French translation: "Le Krausisme espagnol, comme attitude religieuse," *Les Études Philosophiques* (April 1983), pp. 209-216; Juan López Morillas, *El krausismo español* (Mexico: Fondo de Cultura Económica, 1956); *The Krausist Movement and Ideological Change in Spain*, trans. Frances M. López-Morillas (Cambridge, Mass.: Cambridge University Press, 1981); Elías Díaz, *La filosofía social del Krausismo español* (Madrid: Cuadernos para el Diálogo, 1973); Fernando Martín Buezas, *La teología de Sanz del Río y el krausismo español* (Madrid: Editorial Gredos, 1977).

16. Wilhelm Windelband, *Lehrbuch der Geschichte der Philosophie* (Tübingen and Leipzig: J. C. B. Mohr, 1892); 14th ed., revised by Heinz Heimsoeth (Tübingen and Leipzig: J. C. B. Mohr, 1948) and translated by James H. Tufts as *A History of Philosophy* (New York: Macmillan, 1893; 2nd ed. rev. and enl., New York: Macmillan, 1901). [Translator's note]

17. Aloys Müller, *Einleitung in die Philosophie* (Berlin und Bonn: F. Dümmler, 1925). [Translator's note.]

18. José Gaos, *Introducción a la filosofía* (Madrid: Revista de Occidente, *circa* 1934). [Translator's note]

19. The theory that makes psychology the key to philosophy in general. [Editor's note]

20. See José Gaos, "La crítica del psicologismo en Husserl," in *Universidad*, 8 (1931), pp. 3-36; 9 (1932), pp. 625-645; 877-904.

21. Cf. José Gaos, *Confesiones profesionales* (Mexico: Tezontle, 1979), p. 34.

22. See Xavier Zubiri, "Le problème de l'objectivité d'après E. Husserl: I. La logique pure," (Doctoral Thesis, Louvain, 1921, directed by Professor Noël). In the present essay my primary interest resides in the "early" Zubiri, though in Italy he is better known for his mature production. I am referring specifically to Zubiri's "trilogy," namely: *Inteligencia sentiente* (Madrid: Alianza, 1980); *Inteligencia y logos* (Madrid: Alianza, 1982); *Inteligencia y razón* (Madrid: Alianza, 1983). I bear in mind, also, such well-known works as *Cinco lecciones de filosofía* (Madrid: Alianza, 1980). On Zubiri see, among others, these studies by Alain Guy: *Les philosophes espagnols d'hier et d'aujourd'hui*, vol. 1, pp. 233-240, vol. 2 , pp. 170-185; *Los filósofos españoles de ayer y de hoy* (Buenos Aires: Losada, 1966), pp. 182-187; *Historia de la filosofía española* (Barcelona: Anthropos, 1985), pp. 417-425; "X. Zubiri. Notre attitude à l'égard du passé," in *Le temps et la mort dans la philosophie espagnole contemporaine*, ed. A. Guy and A. Serves (Paris and Toulouse: Privat, 1968), pp. 29-48. See, also, Alfonso López Quintás, *Filosofía española contemporánea* (Madrid: Biblioteca de Autores Cristianos, 1970), pp. 196-272; J. Marías, *Filosofía española actual* (Madrid: Espasa-Calpe, 1948), pp. 133-147; Paulino Garagorri, *Unamuno, Ortega, Zubiri en la filosofía española* (Madrid: Editorial Plenitud, 1968), pp. 123-168; Albino Babolin, "La teoria filosofica dell'essenza di X. Zubiri," in *Studi di filosofia in onore di Gustavo Bontadini* (Milan: Vita e Pensiero, 1975), pp. 434-453; Armando Savignano, *Unamuno, Ortega, Zubiri* (Naples: Guida Editori, 1989).

23. Cf. Zubiri, *Ensayo de una teoría fenomenológica del juicio* (Madrid: Revista de Archivos, Bibliotecas y Museos, 1923).

24. Cf. López Quintás, *Filosofía española contemporánea*, p. 200.

25. Ortega's large, multifarious production fills the twelve tomes of his *Obras completas* (Madrid: Revista de Occidente, 1946-1982). Another full volume is taken up by his *Epistolario* (Madrid: Revista de Occidente, 1974). We should recall here his best-known works, published before Franco came to power and, therefore, encompassed within the time-span pertinent to our study: *Meditaciones del Quijote* (Madrid: Residencia de Estudiantes, 1914), translated by E. Rugg and D. Marin as *Meditations on Quixote* (New York: Norton, 1961); *España invertebrada* (Madrid: Espasa-Calpe, 1921), translated by Mildred Adams as *Invertebrate Spain* (New York: Norton, 1937); *Kant, 1724-1924: Reflexiones de centenario* (Madrid: Revista de Occidente, 1929), rpt. as *Kant*, in *Obras completas*, vol. 4 (1947), pp. 25-59; *La deshumanización del arte e ideas sobre la novela* (Madrid: Revista de Occidente, 1925), translated by W. Trask as *The*

Dehumanization of Art (Garden City, N. Y.: Doubleday, 1956); *La rebelión de las masas* (Madrid: Revista de Occidente, 1930), translated by Anthony Kerrigan as *The Revolt of the Masses* (Notre Dame, Ind.: University of Notre Dame Press, 1985); *Rectificación de la República* (Madrid: Revista de Occidente, 1931). A fundamental bibliography on Ortega is contained in these books: Francisco Xavier Pina Prata, *Dialética da raçao vital: Intuiçao originária de José Ortega y Gasset* (Lisbon: Livraria Morais, 1962); J. H. Walgrave, *La filosofía de Ortega y Gasset* (Madrid: Revista de Occidente, 1965); Ciriaco Morón Arroyo, *El sistema de Ortega* (Madrid: Alcalá, 1968); López Quintás, *Filosofía española contemporánea*, pp. 134-137; Guy, *Historia de la filosofía española*, pp. 300-302.

26. Cf. *Meditaciones del Quijote*, 4th ed. (Madrid: Espasa-Calpe, 1982), p. 29.

27. Some critics, A. López Quintás among them, have underscored, with good reason, the importance of "perspectivism" in Ortega's theory of knowledge. López Quintás (*Filosofía española contemporánea*, p. 129) compares Ortega's "doctrine of the point of view" with Husserl's "knowledge through profiles and adumbrations" (cf. Husserl's *Abschattungen*).

28. See Julián Marías, *La Escuela de Madrid* (Buenos Aires: Emecé, 1959) and Ortega's own "Guillermo Dilthey y la idea de la vida," *Revista de Occidente* 125-127 (1933-1944); rpt. in *Obras completas*, vol. 6 (1983), pp. 165-214.

29. See Henri Bergson, *Essai sur les données immédiates de la conscience* (Paris: Félix Alcan, 1889); reprinted in *Oeuvres: Édition du centenaire*, annotated by André Robinet; introduction by Henri Gouthier (Paris: Presses Universitaires de France, 1959); translated by F. L. Pogson as *Time and Free Will: An Essay on the Immediate Data of Consciousness* (New York: Macmillan, 1910).

30. Cf. Ortega's own *Estudios sobre el amor*, first published in 1926-1927.

31. From Manuel García Morente's production, previous to the Spanish Civil War, we will select these titles: *La estética de Kant* (Madrid: Victoriano Suárez, 1912); *La filosofía de Henri Bergson* (Madrid: Residencia de Estudiantes, 1917); *Ensayos sobre el progreso* (Madrid: Imprenta de G. Sáez, 1932); "Sobre la intuición bergsoniana," *Revista General*, 20 (1918), pp. 19-22; "El tema de nuestro tiempo: Filosofía de la perspectiva," *Revista de Occidente*, 5 (1923), pp. 201-217; "Las dos fuentes de la moral y la religión," *Revista de Occidente*, 111 (1932), pp. 270-284. On García Morente himself, see these representative studies, among others: Guy, *Historia de la filosofía española*, pp. 338-342, and "Manuel García Morente ou le bergsonisme chrétien," *Bulletin de la Société des Sciences, Lettres et Arts*, 136 (1980), pp. 265-278; López Quintás, *Filosofía española contemporánea*, pp. 136-150; Luis Aguirre Prado, *García Morente* (Madrid: Servicio de Publicaciones Españoles, 1963); Pedro Muro Romero, *Filosofía, pedagogía e historia en Manuel García Morente* (Madrid: Consejo Superior de Investigaciones Científicas, 1977).

32. Manuel García Morente, *La estética de Kant* (Madrid: V. Suarez, 1912). [Translator's note]

33. Manuel García Morente, *La filosofía de Kant: Una introducción a la filosofía* (Madrid: Espasa-Calpe, 1917). [Translator's note]

34. See M. García Morente, *Fundamentos de Filosofía e Historia de los sistemas filosóficos* (Madrid: Espasa Calpe, 1947), p. 339.

35. *Ibid.*, p. 344.

36. Martin Heidegger, *Was ist Metaphysik?* (Bonn: F. Cohen, 1929). [Translator's note]

37. Werner Jaeger's *Aristoteles: Grundlegung einer Geschichte seiner Entwicklung* (Berlin: Weidmann, 1923), translated by Richard Robinson as *Aristotle, Fundamentals of the History of His Development* (Oxford: Oxford University Press, 1934; 2nd ed., 1948) was published in 1923, but Jaeger's *Studien zur Entstehungsgeschichte der Metaphysik des Aristoteles* (Berlin: Weidmann, 1912) had already appeared in 1912.

38. René Descartes, *Discours de la méthode*, text and commentary by Étienne Gilson, 2d ed. (Paris: 1930). Translated by Elizabeth S. Haldane and G. R. T. Ross as "Discourse on the Method of Rightly Conducting the Reason," in *The Philosophical Works of Descartes*, vol. 1 (Cambridge, England: Cambridge University Press, 1931). [Translator's note]

39. See José Gaos, *De la filosofía* (Mexico: Fondo de Cultura Económica, 1962), p. 465.

40. George Berkeley, "Dialogues between Hylas and Philonous," in A. A. Luce and T. E. Jessop, eds., *The Works of George Berkeley, Bishop of Cloyne*, 9 vols. (London and New York: T. Nelson, 1948-1957). [Translator's note]

41. *Religación* is the bond that unites us to the transcendence, to God. "The human being does not have religion," writes Zubiri, "he consists in 'religación' or 'religion.'" See Zubiri, "En torno al problema de Dios," *Revista de Occidente*, 149 (1935), pp. 129-159; reprinted in Zubiri, *Naturaleza, historia, Dios* (Madrid: Editora Nacional, 5th ed., 1963), pp. 361-397. Apropos of this theme, see A. Guy "La théorie de la religation selon Xavier Zubiri," Bordeaux, *Bulletin Hispanique*, 66:3-4 (1964), pp. 391-395.

42. Gaos, *Confesiones*, pp. 56-57.

43. Martin Heidegger, *El ser y el tiempo*, translated into Spanish by José Gaos (Mexico: Fondo de Cultura Económica, 1951). The book features a prologue and an index of key terms in the Spanish translation. Also in 1951, the same publisher put out Gaos's opuscule, *Introducción a "El ser y el tiempo" de Martin Heidegger*. Martin Heidegger's *Sein und Zeit*, 7th ed. (Tübingen: Neomarius Verlag, 1953) has been translated into English by John Macquarrie and Edward Robinson (New York and Evanston: Harper & Row, 1962). [Translator's note]

44. Martin Heidegger, *Über den Humanismus* (Frankfurt a. M.: V. Klostermann, 1947). [Translator's note]

45. Cf. Gaos, *Confesiones*, p. 59.

46. Karl Jaspers, *Existenzphilosophie*. Three lectures given at the Freie Hochstift in Frankfurt am Main, in September 1937 (Berlin and Leipzig: W. de Gruyter and Co., 1938); 2nd enlarged ed. (with postscript), 1956.

47. Karl Jaspers, *Existenzphilosophie*, translated into Spanish by José Gaos, "La filosofía desde el punto de vista de la existencia," *Breviario del Fondo de Cultura Económica* 77 (Mexico: 1953). [Translator's note]

48. Karl Jaspers, *Philosophie*, 3 vols. (Berlin: J. Springer, 1932). [Translator's note]

49. No need to reconsider here, in its historical significance, the revolt of the Carlists, the so-called "legitimists," which was provoked by the decision of Fernando VII, Don Carlos's brother, to abolish the Salic law. This law has barred the succession of the female line to the throne. Fernando was paving the way for the succession of his own daughter, Isabel (later, Isabel II). [Translator's note]

50. Fernando de los Ríos y Urruti, *El sentido humano del socialismo* (Madrid: J. Morata, 1926). [Translator's note]

51. It is appropriate to report Gaos's words in full:

> And the Republic came into being! What days of celebration, the likes of which were never put on before and were never to be seen again! Take a man most averse to mix with others: Will he not feel a compulsion to do just about anything in those moments of immense excitement in the community? To come to the point, take even a fellow like myself: at times, while perched on top of a taxicab, I roused the crowd and, at other times, I asked people to stay calm and orderly; from the top of a taxicab, mind you! Then the root of the vehicle caved in, and Santiago Pi Suñer, a professor at the Medical School, and yours truly came tumbling down, inside the car, not without torn muscles, scrapes, and bruises. The experiences of those days were truly unique, never to be forgotten. . . . Above all, and I mean above all, the joy born of hope, the glorious, tearful joy of seeing myriad brown-striped flags flutter high and low, large and small, in the April breeze of Zaragoza's sky. I wish I could convey a mere inkling of the emotion I felt. It was of a kind that I had never experienced before and I have not experienced since; this social, patriotic, civic euphoria. I wish I could enable you to feel it as I felt it, as I relive it even now. Had I the skills of a gifted writer, I would transport you from the Zaragoza of 1931 to the Cádiz of 1810. (*Confesiones*, p. 108)

52. Cf. Ortega y Gasset, *Rectificación de la República*.

53. Cf. José Gaos, "Los 'transterrados' españoles de la filosofía en México," *Filosofía y Letras: Revista de la Universidad de México*, 36 (October-December, 1949). See Francisco Romero, *Ortega y Gasset y el problema de la jefatura espiritual* (Buenos Aires: Losada, 1960), p. 30, where Romero states that "'destierro' is the natural condition of the Spanish philosophers." To the contrary, Gaos, in describing the condition of his fellow refugees in Mexico, does not call them *desterrados* (depatriated), exiles, that is, uprooted at the deepest level, deprived of their homeland. He calls them, instead, *transterrados* (cross-patriated) and coins, thereby, a term, much stronger than the Italian *trasferiti* (transposed). In this respect, José Luis Abellán reminds us:

> In this identification with the Mexican nation, Gaos aims at formulating his own theory of the two countries: one "of origin," is assigned to us by circumstances that transcend personal decision; and the country "of destiny," freely chosen, because it coincides with the life plan to which we voluntarily have committed ourselves. (J. L. Abellán, *Panorama de la filosofía española actual: Una situación escandalosa* [Madrid: Espasa Calpe, 1978], p. 123.)

54. For additional details concerning the publication of these volumes, see the bibliography appended to this work.

55. Gaos, *Confesiones*, p. 148.

56. See the general bibliography appended to this work.

57. See José Gaos, *Dos exclusivas del hombre: La mano y el tiempo* (Veracruz, Mexico: Universidad de Nuevo León, 1945).

Chapter Two

58. José Gaos, *De la filosofía* (Mexico: Fondo de Cultura Económica, 1962); *Del hombre* (Mexico: Fondo de Cultura Económica, 1970).

59. Gaos, *Del hombre*, p. 22.

60. *Ibid.*

61. *Suppositio* is a property of a term as expressed in a proposition. The *suppositio*, as distinguished from the *significatio*, refers to what the term "stands-for." The *significatio* refers to the relation between a sign and the thing signified. [Editor's note]

62. Gaos, *Del hombre*, p. 142.

63. Gaos, *De la filosofía*, p. 204.

64. *Ibid.*, p. 234.

Chapter Three

65. Colonnello uses the Italian word *ente* from the Latin *ens*. [Translator's note]

66. Martin Heidegger, *Sein und Zeit* (Halle: Max Niemeyer, 1937; 3rd ed., 1931), p. 38; *Being and Time*, trans. John Macquarrie and Edward Robinson (New York and Evanston, Ill.: Harper & Row, 1962), Int. II, ¶ 7, p. 62.

67. Gaos, *De la filosofía*, p. 255.

68. *Ibid.*, pp. 256-257.

69. Here and for the other "being" that follows immediately, Colonnello uses the Latin infinitive *essere* (to be). [Translator's note]

70. In Italian the adjective *gnoseologico* refers to post-Berkelean epistemology. [Editor's note]

71. Gaos, *De la filosofía*, p. 462.

72. Gaos, *Del hombre*, p. 325.

73. Colonnello uses the Italian word *enti* referring to the plural manifestation of the *ens*. [Translator's note]

74. Gaos, *De la filosofía*, p. 223.

75. *Ibid.*, p. 375.

76. *Ibid.*, p. 376.

77. *Ibid.*, p. 320.

78. Heidegger, *Sein und Zeit*, pp. 280-289; and *Being and Time*, Part One, Division Two, ¶ 58, pp. 325-335.

79. Aristotle, "De Interpretatione," trans. E. M. Edghill, 17a, 26, in *The Works of Aristotle*, eds. J. A. Smith and W. D. Ross (Oxford: Oxford University Press, 1928), vol. 1.

80. Here we come upon a problem taken up on various occasions in the history of Western thought. Of particular interest, since it has a direct bearing upon our discussion, is Kant's treatment of the logical function of the intellect in statements. Kant takes the opportunity to draw distinctions among affirmative, negative, and infinitive statements. Remarkable too is what he writes about the need to distinguish between the two sentences: "The soul is not mortal" and "The soul is not-mortal." See I. Kant, *Kritik der reinen Vernunft*, B 95-97; and *Critique of Pure Reason*, trans. Norman Kemp Smith (New York: St. Martin's Press; Toronto: Macmillan, 1965), p. 108. It is tempting to take a look at an historical issue such as Gaos's reading of Kant (a topic to which I shall

return); or, to name another possibility, we could test the originality of Gaos's theory and verify his position under discussion here. An excursion into Kantian territory would lead us far afield from our main subject.

81. Gaos, *De la filosofía*, p. 329.

82. Gaos, *Del hombre*, p. 343.

83. *Ibid.*, p. 345.

Chapter Four

84. The Greek phrase means, literally, "to give word," "to provide reason." [Translator's note]

85. "Me-ontology" (*meontologia*) refers to the philosophy of non-being. [Translator's note]

86. Gaos, *De la filosofía*, p. 385.

87. *Ibid.*, p. 388.

88. *Ibid.*, p. 391.

89. *Ibid.*, p. 398.

90. *Ibid.* Cf. Immanuel Kant, *Critique of Pure Reason*, B 454-B 471.

91. Gaos, *De la filosofía*, p. 412.

92. *Ibid.*

93. I do not insist here on a complete exposition, nor do I strive, in good historiographical form, for a *restitutio ad integrum* of the text of the *Critique of Pure Reason*. Nevertheless, the weight of the coincidences between Kant's and Gaos's theories obliges us to take notice of one thorny problem in the interpretation of Kant's antinomies. Specifically, with regard to the third antinomy, the following issues remain to be bolstered by sufficient evidence: (1) how transcendental liberty is to be installed at the foundation of practical liberty and of morality in general; (2) how, consequently, the positive meaning of metaphysics resides in the survival of metaphysics not only as a rational science of nature but also as a rational science of human conduct; (3) how the problem of the unconditional—the problem of the rejection of metaphysics as a product of speculative reason—turns out to be not just one problem among many, but the crucial question of the entire system of transcendental philosophy.

94. Gaos, *De la filosofía*, p. 415.

95. *Ibid.*, p. 418.

96. Colonnello uses the adjective *entitativa* in reference to the *antinomia della finitudine e della infinitudine*. [Translator's note]

97. *Entitativamente* in Colonnello's terminology. [Translator's note]

98. Gaos, *De la filosofía*, p. 419.

99. The neologisms used by Colonnello are *finitismo* and *infinitismo*. [Translator's note]

100. Gaos, *Del hombre*, p. 477.

101. *Ibid.*

102. Cf. Saint Thomas Aquinas, *Summa theologica*, I, qu. 5, a. 1; qu. 5, a. 3.

103. Kant, *Critique of Pure Reason*, B 347.

104. Gaos, *Del hombre*, pp. 478-479.

105. *Ibid.*, p. 480.

106. *Ibid.*, p. 484.

Chapter Five

107. Here and elsewhere Gaos uses the term *hombre* (and Colonnello uses the Italian term *uomo*) to the refer to the human genus, "man" or "mankind," which refers both to female as well as male individuals. In present-day formal English we would use the non-gender terms "humanity" or "human beings," and I have generally used these to translate Colonnello's *uomo* and Gaos's *hombre*. [Editor's note]

108. Gaos, *De la filosofía*, p. 430.

109. See Gianni Vattimo, "La crisi della soggettività da Nietzsche a Heidegger," in *La crisi del soggetto nel pensiero contemporaneo*, ed. A. Bruno (Milan: Angeli, 1988), p. 62. In the same volume also of great interest are the essays by C. Cesa, G. Bedeschi, E. Funari, F. Fellmann, A. Bruno, S. Zecchi, G. Cotroneo, F. Bianco, C. Sini, R. Franchini, S. Nicolosi.

110. Vattimo, "La crisi della soggettività," pp. 62-63.

111. Taken in its narrow sense, the Italian term *apodissi* refers to demonstration or to a syllogism that deduces a conclusion from first and true principles, or from other propositions deduced syllogistically from first and self-evident principles. Colonnello, however, uses *apodissi* in its wide sense, that is as referring to the essence of science and equivalent to formal rigor, to rational certainty. The necessity and the cogency of philosophical rationality is reflected also in the adjective *apodittico*, which beyond the meaning of "demonstrative," also assumes the meaning of "necessary," as in Kant's *apodittici* judgments and Husserl's *apodittica* proof. [Editor's note]

112. Kant, *Critique of Pure Reason*, §27.

113. One of the most incisive definitions of affect exists in Aristotle, who puts the center of what is psychical in *pathos* (passion), understood as every emotion of the soul, such as appetite, fear, joy, longing, hatred, pity, which are accompanied by pleasure or pain. See Aristotle, *Ethica Nicomachea*, ed. W. D. Ross, vol. 9, *The Works of Aristotle translated into English* (London: Oxford University Press, 1954), 2, 1105 b 21-25; see also *De anima*, vol. 3, *ibid.*, 403 b 25-26 and *De Interpretatione*, vol. 1, *ibid.*, 16 b 26-27. The passions of the soul are neither the virtues nor the vices. They are not determined by a conscious choice: we feel anger and fear without choice, but the virtues are modes of choice or involve choice (*Ethica Nicomachea*, 2, 1106 a 1-5). The emotions of the soul represent instead the immediate reactions of the living; reactions of emotive or sentimental order, to situations at times favorable or unfavorable to the individual.

114. See Kant, "Transcendental Aesthetic," *Critique of Pure Reason*, Sec. 2, §8, B 66.

115. See Aldo Masullo, "Soggetto 'patico' e fine del trascendentale," *Paradigmi*, 6 (1988), p. 165, note 16. See also by the same author, *Filosofia del soggetto e diritto del senso* (Genoa: Marietti, 1990), pp. 177-214; "Il fondamento e il tempo" in *Il problema del fondamento e la filosofia italiana del Novecento*, ed. P. Ciaravolo (Rome: Publicazioni del Centro per la Filosofia Italiana, 1992), pp. 7-28; *Struttura, Soggetto, Prassi* (Naples: Edizioni Scientifiche Italiane, 1994); *Il tempo e la grazia. Per un'etica della salvezza* (Rome: Donzelli, 1995).

116. Cf. Dilthey, *Einleitung in die Geistewissenschaften. Versuch einer Grundlegung für das Studium der Gesellschaft und der Geschichte*, in *Gesammelte Schriften* (Leipzig: hrsg. von B. Groethuysen, Teubner, 1922; 8th ed. Stuttgart-Göttingen, 1979), vol. 1:

In the veins of the cognitive subject constructed by Locke, Hume, and Kant, real blood does not run; but the rarefied lymph of a reason understood as pure activity of thought. As historian and psychologist, I had to deal with the entire human being and was led to assume, for a base, this being in the multiplicity of human forces, this willing, feeling, and representing being. I did so also when explaining knowledge and its concepts (as external world, time, substance, cause). Knowledge, however, seems to elaborate these concepts only by starting from the material of perceiving, representing, and thinking.

117. Cf. W. Dilthey, *Plan der Fortsetzung zum Aufbau der geschichtlichen Welt in den Geisteswissenschaften* in *Gesammelte Schriften* (Leipzig: hrsg. von B. Groethuysen, Teubner, 1927; 7th ed. Stuttgart-Göttingen, 1979), vol. 7.

118. W. Dilthey, *Grundlegung der Wissenschaften vom Menschen, der Gesellschaft und der Geschichte*, in *Gesammelte Schriften* (Göttingen: hrsg. von H. Johach und F. Rodi, Vandenhoeck und Ruprecht, 1982), vol. 19, p. 44.

119. Cf. Heidegger, *Sein und Zeit*, p. 377; *Being and Time*, Part 1, Division 2.5, ¶ 72, p. 429.

120. Kant, *Kritik der reinen Vernunft*, B 137.

121. See Heidegger, *Sein und Zeit*, p. 146; *Being and Time*, Part 1, Division 1.5, ¶ 31, p. 186.

122. The German term *Befindlichkeit* is translated into Italian by *situazione emotiva, tonalità affettiva*, or the expression *il sentirsi situato*, which best describes the state in which Being-there (*Dasein*) finds itself insofar as it is a thrown-being. For this reason, I suggest that *situazione emotiva* be translated into English as "ontological disposition." [Author's note added to the English translation of this text]

123. Heidegger, *Sein und Zeit*, p. 139; *Being and Time*, Part 1, Division 1.5, ¶ 29, pp. 178-179.

124. Cf. Aldo Masullo, *Soggetto "patico" e fine del transcendentale*, pp. 184ff.

125. Gaos, *Del hombre*, p. 523.

126. *Ibid.*

127. *Ibid.*, p. 524.

128. *Ibid.*, p. 525.

129. *Ibid.*, p. 527.

130. *Ibid.*, p. 529.

131. *Ibid.*

132. *Ibid.*

133. *Ibid.*, p. 530.

134. *Ibid.*

135. *Ibid.*, p. 534.

136. *Ibid.*, p. 545.

137. *Ibid.*, p. 554.

138. *Ibid.*, p. 572.

139. *Ibid.*, pp. 574-575.

140. Gaos, *De la filosofia*, pp. 463-464.

141. *Ibid.*, p. 471.

Chapter Six

142. See J. Gaos, *Dos exclusivas del hombre: La mano y el tiempo* (Mexico: Fondo de Cultura Económica, 1945).

143. *Ibid.*, p. 21.

144. *Ibid.*, p. 114.

145. *Ibid.*, p. 117.

146. *Ibid.*, p. 121.

147. *Ibid.*, p. 123.

148. *Ibid.*, p. 130.

149. *Ibid.*, p. 132.

150. Colonnello coins the verb *presentificare*. In English, the corresponding verb is "presentiate," that is, "to make present," which has become obsolete. [Translator's note]

151. Gaos uses the expressions *cuasicosas* and *quisicosas* to designate the things produced by abstraction.

152. Gaos, *Dos exclusivas del hombre*, p. 142.

153. Cf. *ibid.*, p. 148, where Gaos writes:

> Hay en el lenguaje corriente ciertas expresiones que lo son de *una relación entre el hombre y el tiempo que no se da entre ningún otro ser o cosa y el tiempo*. Tener tiempo, hacer tiempo, ganar o perder tiempo, perder el tiempo, pasar el tiempo, matar el tiempo y alguna más. [In ordinary speech there are some expressions that are such because of *a relationship between man and time, a relationship which does not occur between any other being or thing and time*. These expressions are: to have time, to make time, to gain or lose time, to waste time, to pass the time, to kill time, and some others.]

154. *Ibid.*, p. 149.

155. See *ibid.*, p. 159:

> Only the consciousness of our finitude, of the limit that is imposed upon the duration of our lives, stimulates the human being to "occupy time" ("hacer tiempo"). If we are capable of acting, it is precisely because we are limited by death: "because we are mortal, finite, temporal in the most appropriate sense of the word." Besides, if death is a typically human condition, it is because the human being is the most temporal of the beings. The human being is the entity, the beginning from which the scene or the horizon of time is displayed.

156. Aristotle, *Physica*, IV, 11, 219 b 1 in *The Works of Aristotle*, ed. Sir David Ross (Oxford: Clarendon Press, 1953), vol. 2.

157. René Descartes, *Principles of Philosophy*, Part 1, principle 57, in *Philosophical Works of Descartes*, trans. Elizabeth Haldane and G. R. T. Ross (Dover, 1955), vol. 1, p. 242.

158. Immanuel Kant, *Critique of Pure Reason*, trans. Norman Kemp Smith (New York: St Martin's Press; Toronto: Macmillan, 1965), p. 218.

159. *Ibid.*, B 238, p. 222.

160. St. Augustine, *The Confessions*, trans. R. S. Pine-Coffin (Baltimore: Penguin Books, 1961), Book 11, Ch. 28, p. 276.

161. E. Husserl, *Zur Phänomenologie des Inneren Zeitbewusstseins* (The Hague: Nijhoff, 1966), p. 23.

162. Heidegger, *Being and Time*, Division 2.3, ¶ 65, p. 372.

163. *Ibid.*, p. 373.

164. *Ibid.*, p. 479.

165. Cf. Giacomo Marramao, *Minima temporalia: Tempo, spazio, esperienza* (Milan: Il Saggiatore, 1990), p. 127.

166. *Ibid.*

167. See G. W. F. Hegel, *Encyclopädie der philosophischen Wissenschaften in Grundrisse* (Leipzig: Verlag der Dürr'schen Buchhandlung, 1905), §§254-260; *Encyclopedia of the Philosophical Sciences*, §§ 254-260.

168. Colonnello uses the term *significato*. [Translator's note]

169. This quotation and the longer one that follows is taken from Giacomo Leopardi's "L'infinito," one of the greatest Italian poems of all time. [Translator's note]

170. These verses conclude Leopardi's prodigious poem, "L'infinito." [Translator's note]

BIBLIOGRAPHY

1. Works by José Gaos
(In Chronological Order)

La crítica del psicologismo en Husserl. Zaragoza, 1933.

La filosofía de Maimónides. Mexico City: La Casa de España, 1940.

Dos ideas de la filosofía. Mexico City: La Casa de España, 1940. [In collaboration with F. Larroyo]

El pensamiento hispanoamericano. Mexico City: Colegio de México, 1944.

Dos exclusivas del hombre: La mano y el tiempo. Veracruz, Mexico: Universidad de Nuevo León, 1945.

Filosofía de la filosofía e historia de la filosofía. Mexico City: Stylo, 1947.

Pensamiento de lengua española. Mexico City: Stylo, 1947.

El encuentro de Oriente y Occidente. 1948.

"Los 'transterrados' españoles de la filosofía en México." *Filosofía y Letras: Revista de la Universidad de México,* 36 (1949): 207-231.

"Un método para resolver los problemas de nuestro tiempo (la filosofía de P. Northrop)." *Cuadernos Americanos* (1949): 87-111.

"De paso por el historicismo y el existencialismo." *Revista de la Facultad de Filosofía y Letras* (1951): 43-44.

Introducción a "El ser y el tiempo" de Martin Heidegger. Mexico City: Fondo de Cultura Económica, 1951.

En torno a la filosofía mexicana. Mexico City: Porrúa y Obregón, 1952-1953.

Filosofía mexicana de nuestros días. Mexico City: Universidad Nacional Autónoma de México, 1954.

La filosofía en la universidad. Mexico City: Universidad Nacional Autónoma de México, 1956.

Diez por ciento. Mexico City: Tezontle, 1957.

Sobre Ortega y Gasset y otros trabajos de historia de las ideas en España y la América española. Mexico City: Universidad Nacional Autónoma de México, 1957.

La filosofía en la universidad. Ejemplos y complementos. Mexico City: Universidad Nacional Autónoma de México, 1958.

Confesiones profesionales. Mexico City: Fondo de Cultura Económica, 1958.

Discurso de filosofía y otros trabajos sobre la materia. Xalapa, Mexico: Universidad Veracruzana, 1959.

Introducción a la fenomenología, seguida de la crítica del psicologismo en Husserl. Xalapa, Mexico: Universidad Veracruzana, 1960.

Sobre la enseñanza y educación. Mexico City: University of Mexico imprint, 1960.

Orígenes de la filosofía y su historia. Xalapa, Mexico: Universidad Veracruzana, 1960.

De la filosofía. Mexico City: Fondo de Cultura Económica, 1962.

Doce por ciento. Río Piedras: Universidad de Puerto Rico, 1962.

Filosofía contemporánea. Caracas: Universidad Central de Venezuela, Ediciones de la Biblioteca, 1962.

La "Críticas" de Kant. Caracas: Universidad Central de Venezuela, Ediciones de la Biblioteca, 1962.

De antropología e historia. Cuadernos de la Facultad de Filosofía, Letras y Ciencias, 40. Xalapa, Mexico: Universidad Veracruzana, 1967.

Del hombre. Mexico City: Fondo de Cultura Económica, 1970.

Confesiones profesionales. Mexico City: Tezontle, 1979.

Obras completas, 19 volumes. 9 vols. (2, 5, 6, 7, 9, 12, 13, 14, 17) to date, 2 vols. (4, 8) in press. Mexico City: Universidad Nacional Autónoma de México, 1982-.

"Confesiones de transterrado." *Revista de la Universidad Nacional Autónoma de México*, 49 (June 1994): 3-9.

"Seis Cartas Inéditas." *Revista de la Universidad Nacional Autónoma de México*, 49 (June 1994): 33-39.

Gaos, José, and Antonio Moxó. "La cátedra de Pedagogía." *Revista de la Universidad Nacional Autónoma de México*, 49 (June 1994): 45-48.

2. Anthologies and Editions by José Gaos
(In Chronological Order)

Antología filosófica. La filosofía griega. Edited and translated by José Gaos. Mexico City: La Casa de España en México, 1941.

Pensamiento español. Biblioteca Enciclopédica Popular, 56. Mexico City: Secretaría de Educación Pública, 1945.

Antología del pensamiento de lengua española en la edad contemporánea (1744-1944). Colección Laberinto, 5. Mexico City: Editorial Séneca, 1945.

Díaz de Gamarra, J. B. *Tratados*. Biblioteca del Estudiante Universitario, 65. Mexico City: Universidad Nacional Autónoma de México, 1947.

Bello, Andrés. *Filosofía del entendimiento*. Colección Americana. Mexico City: Fondo de Cultura Económica, 1948.

Escritores místicos españoles. Clásicos Jackson, 28. Buenos Aires: Jackson, 1949.

3. Translations by José Gaos
(In Chronological Order)

Messer, August. *La filosofía en el siglo XIX empirismo y naturalismo*. Madrid: Revista de Occidente, 1931. From German.

Müller, Aloys. *Introducción a la filosofía*. Madrid: Revista de Occidente, *circa* 1934. From German.

Los fragmentos de Heráclito. Mexico City: Alcancía, 1939. From Greek.

Husserl, Edmund. *Meditaciones cartesianas*. Con prólogo y notas. Colección de Textos Clásicos de Filosofía, 4. Mexico City: El Colegio de México, 1942. From German.

Odebrecht, Rudolf. *La estética contemporánea. Anales del Instituto de Investigaciones Estéticas*, 8 (suplemento). Mexico City: Universidad Nacional Autónoma de México, 1942. From German.

Scheler, Max. *Esencia y formas de simpatía*. Biblioteca Filosófica. Buenos Aires: Losada, 1943. From German.

Gröthuysen, Bernhard. *La formación de la conciencia burguesa en Francia durante el siglo XVIII*. Colección de obras históricas. I. Los grandes estudios. Mexico City: Fondo de Cultura Económica, 1943. From French.

Dilthey, Wilhelm. *Leibniz y su tiempo*. In *De Leibniz a Goethe*, by W. Dilthey. Mexico City: Fondo de Cultura Económica, 1945. From German.

Jaeger, Werner. *Aristóteles: Bases para la historia de su desarrollo intelectual.* Mexico City: Fondo de Cultura Económica, 1946. From German.

Dewey, John. *La experiencia y la naturaleza.* Mexico City: Fondo de Cultura Económica, 1948. From English.

Husserl, Edmund. *Ideas relativas a una fenomenología pura y una filosofía fenomenológica.* Mexico City: Fondo de Cultura Económica, 1949. From German.

Wahl, J. *Introducción a la filosofía.* Breviarios del Fondo de Cultura Económica, 34. Mexico City: Fondo de Cultura Económica, 1951. From French.

Heidegger, Martin. *El ser y el tiempo.* Mexico City: Fondo de Cultura Económica, 1952. From German.

Jaeger, Werner. *La teología de los primeros filósofos griegos.* Mexico City: Fondo de Cultura Económica, 1952. From German.

Jaspers, Karl. *La filosofía desde el punto de vista de la existencia.* Breviario del Fondo de Cultura Económica, 77. Mexico City: Fondo de Cultura Económica, 1953. From German.

Lavelle, Louis. *Introducción a la ontología.* Mexico City: Fondo de Cultura Económica, 1953. From French.

Abbagnano, Nicola. *Introducción al existencialismo.* Mexico City: Fondo de Cultura Económica, 1953. From Italian.

Hartmann, Nicolai. *Ontología I: Fundamentos.* Mexico City: Fondo de Cultura Económica, 1956. From German.

———. *Ontología II: Posibilidades y efectividad.* Mexico City: Fondo de Cultura Económica, 1956. From German.

———. *Ontología III: La fábrica del mundo real.* Mexico City: Fondo de Cultura Económica, 1959. From German.

———. *Ontología IV: Filosofía de la naturaleza. Teoría especial de las categorías. Categorías dimensionales. Categorías cosmológicas.* Mexico City: Fondo de Cultura Económica, 1960. From German.

———. *Ontología V: El pensar teleológico.* Mexico City: Fondo de Cultura Económica, 1964. From German.

Heimsoeth, Heinz. *Los seis grandes temas de la metafísica occidental.* 2nd ed. Madrid: Revista de Occidente, 1965. From German.

Huizinga, Johan. *El otoño de la Edad Media*. 6th ed. Madrid: Revista de Occidente, 1965. From German.

Spranger, Eduard. *Psicología de la edad juvenil*. 7th ed. Madrid: Revista de Occidente, 1965. From German.

Fichte, Johann Gottlieb. *Los caracteres de la edad contemporánea*. Madrid: Revista de Occidente, 1965. From German.

Hessen, Johannes. *Teoría del conocimiento*. 15th ed. Madrid: Espasa-Calpe, 1979. From German.

Hegel, Georg Wilhelm Friedrich. *Lecciones sobre la filosofía de la historia universal*. Madrid: Alianza, 1980. From German.

4. Critical Literature on José Gaos

Abellán, José Luis. *De la guerra civil al exilio republicano (1936-1977)*. Madrid: Mezquita, 1983.

————. *Filosofía española en América (1936-1955)*, 103-122. Madrid: Guadarrama, 1966.

————. "La contribución de José Gaos a la historia de las ideas en Hispanoamérica." *Diánoia*, 16 (1970): 205-231.

————. *Panorama de la filosofía española actual: Una situación escandalosa*, 110-113, 122-123. Madrid: Espasa-Clape, 1978.

Alvarenga, José Luis. "Entrevista en Caracas con José Gaos." *Indice* (June 1959).

Aranguren, José Luis. "Expresiones verbales y expresiones filosóficas en el contexto 'De la filosofía.'" *Diánoia*, 16 (1970): 157-163.

Ardao, Arturo. "Lenguaje, lengua y filosofía en Gaos." *Revista Venezolana de Filosofía*, 18: 7-17.

Brun, J. L. *Prendre et comprendre: Essais sur les rapports de la main et de l'esprit*. Paris: Presses universitaires de France, 1963.

Cardiel Reyes, Raúl. "Filosofía de la filosofía." *Cuadernos Americanos* (September-October 1969): 45-58.

Fernández, J. "Carta de José Gaos a Julio Montes." *Cuadernos Americanos* (September-October 1969): 59-68.

————. "Una indagación estética de José Gaos." *Diánoia*, 16 (1970): 253-264.

Ferrater Mora, José. "Gaos." *Diccionario de filosofía*. 3rd ed. Buenos Aires: Editorial Sudamericana, 1965.

Gómez Roblero, A. "Mis recuerdos de Gaos." *Cuadernos Americanos* (September-October 1969): 69-73.

Guerra, Alfonso Rangel. "Cartas de José Gaos." *Revista de la Universidad Nacional Autónoma de México*, 49 (June 1994): 31-32.

Guy, Alain. "El tiempo en la filosofía de J. Gaos." *Diánoia*, 16 (1970): 172-186.

————. *Historia de la filosofía española*, 315-320. Barcelona: Anthropos, 1985.

————. *Histoire de la philosophie espagnole*. Toulouse: Association des Publications de l'Université de Toulouse-Le Mirail, 1983.

————. "La fenomenología de la caricia y de la muerte en J. Gaos." *Humanitas* (1963): 97-113.

————. "La langage de la caresse selon J. Gaos," 197-203. XII Congresso di Filosofia. Venice, 1958.

————. "La temporalité et la mort selon J. Gaos." In *Pensée et finitude*, 17-40. Toulouse: Université de Toulouse-Le Mirail.

————. *Les philosophes espagnols d'hier et d'aujourd'hui*. Toulouse: Privat, 1956. 1, pp. 241-249; 2, pp. 185-194.

————, trans. "Les temps, dimension essentielle de l'homme." By José Gaos. In *Les temps et la mort dans la philosophie espagnole contemporaine*, 107-129. Toulouse: Privat, 1968.

————. *Los filósofos españoles de ayer y de hoy*, 188-190, 301-302. Buenos Aires: Losada, 1966.

Hernández Luna, Juan. "En torno a un curso sobre el historicismo del maestro José Gaos." *Cuadernos Americanos* (September-October 1969): 74-80.

Izquierdo Ortega, Julio. "De la filosofía." *Indice* (March 1965).

Larroyo, Francisco. "El filosofar de José Gaos en exposición genética." *Cuadernos Americanos* (September-October 1969): 81-101.

López Quintás, Alfonso. *Filosofía española contemporánea*, 182-185. Madrid: Biblioteca de Autores Cristianos, 1970.

Muñoz Alonso, Adolfo. *Las grandes corrientes del pensamiento contemporáneo*, 395-396. Madrid: Guadarrama, 1959.

Navarro, B. "El pensamiento griego en la obra de José Gaos." *Diánoia*, 16 (1970): 232-252.

Nicol, Eduardo. "Otra idea de la filosofía: Respuesta a José Gaos." *Cuadernos Americanos* (May-June 1951).

Rodríguez Neira, Teófilo. "José Gaos: La idea del mundo." *El basilisco* (Oviedo) (1983-1984).

Romanelli, Pietro. "Tributo a José Gaos." *Diánoia*, 16 (1970): 288-292.

Rukser, Udo. "José Gaos: Sobre 'El origen y la historia de la filosofía.'" *Diánoia*, 16 (1970): 187-204.

Salazar Bondy, Augusto. "Un tema de Gaos: Abstracción y verdad." *Diánoia*, 16 (1970): 164-171.

Salazar, R., and E. Bustamante. "Bibliografía del filósofo José Gaos (1900-1969)." In *Libro anual (1971-1972)*, 223-259. Mexico City: Instituto Superior de Estudios Eclesiásticos, 1971-1972.

Salmerón, Fernando. "José Gaos: Su idea de la filosofía." *Cuadernos Americanos* (September-October 1969): 102-129.

————. "La naturaleza humana y la razón de ser de la filosofía." *Diánoia*, 20 (1974): 147-171.

————. "Sobre el pensamento de José Gaos. La filosofía política de los Transterrados." *Revista de la Universidad Nacional Autónoma de México*, 49 (June 1994): 10-18.

Sánchez Villaseñor, José. *Gaos en Mascarones: La crisis del historicismo y otros ensayos*. Mexico City: Jus, 1945.

Sichez Recaséns, J. "Gaos y J. Ortega y Gasset." *Diánoia*, 16 (1970): 79-87.

Uranga, Emilio. "José Gaos: Personalidad y confesión." *Cuadernos Americanos* (September-October 1969): 130-156.

Villoro, Luis. "La filosofía de José Gaos." *Diánoia*, 10 (1964).

Xirau, Ramón. "José Gaos o del valer la pena." *Cuadernos Americanos* (September-October 1969): 157-164.

————. "De Descartes a Marx. La historia de la filosofía en la obra de José Gaos." *Revista de la Universidad Nacional Autónoma de México*, 49 (June 1994): 40-44.

Yamuni Tabush, Vera. "La autobiografía filosófica de José Gaos." *Diánoia*, 16 (1970): 265-278.

Zea, Leopoldo. "José Gaos y la filosofía mexicana." *Cuadernos Americanos* (September-October 1969): 165-175.

———. "La filosofía mexicana de José Gaos." *Revista de la Universidad Nacional Autónoma de México*, 49 (June 1994): 19-25.

5. Recommended Works on Spanish and Hispanic-American Philosophical Culture of José Gaos's Time

Abellán, José Luis. *La cultura en España*. Madrid: Edicusa, 1971.

———. *Panorama de la filosofía española actual: Una situación escandalosa*. Madrid: Espasa-Calpe, 1978.

Aguirre Prado, Luis. *García Morente*. Madrid: 1963.

Alonso Fueyo, Sabino. *Filosofía y narcisismo: En torno a los pensadores de la España actual*. Valencia: Editorial Guerri, 1953.

Babolin, Albino. "La teoria filosofica dell'essenza di X. Zubiri." In *Studi di filosofia in onore di Gustavo Bontadini*. 2 vols. Milan: Vita e Pensiero, 1975.

Baker, Armand F. "The God of Miguel de Unamuno." *Hispania*, 74 (1991): 824-833.

Brenan, Gerald. *The Spanish Labyrinth: An Account of the Social and Political Background of the Civil War*. Cambridge, England: The Cambridge University Press, 1960.

Casanovas, Ignasi. *Balmes: La seva vida, el seu temps, les seves obres*. Barcelona: Biblioteca Balmes, 1932.

Ceñal, P. R. "La filosofía española contemporánea." In *Actas del I Congreso Nacional de Filosofía. Mendoza, Argentina: Marzo 30-Abril 9, 1949*, 423-426. Buenos Aires: Platt, Establecimientos Gráficos, 1950.

De los Ríos y Urruti, Fernando. *El sentido humano del socialismo*. Madrid: J. Morata, 1926.

Díaz, Elías. *La filosofía social del krausismo español*. Madrid: Editorial Cuadernos para el Diálogo, 1973.

———. *Pensamiento español 1939-1973*. Madrid: Edicusa, 1974.

Ferran, Jaime, and Daniel P. Testa, eds. *Spanish Writers of 1936 (Crisis and Commitment in the Poetry of the Thirties and Forties): An Anthology of Literary Studies and Essays*. London: Tamesis, 1973.

Garagorri, Paulino. *Unamuno, Ortega, Zubiri en la filosofía española*. Madrid: Editorial Plenitud, 1968.

García Bacca, Juan David. *Antropología filosófica contemporánea*. Barcelona: Anthropos, 1982.

————. "El sentido de la nada en la fundamentación de la metafísica según Heidegger, y el sentido de la nada como fundamentación de la experiencia mística según San Juan de la Cruz." *Cuadernos Americanos* (November-December 1944).

————. *Existencialismo*. Xalapa, Mexico: Universidad Veracruzana, 1962.

————. "Existencialismo alemán y existencialismo francés: Heidegger y Sartre." *Cuadernos Americanos* (July-August 1947).

García Morente, Manuel. "El tema de nuestro tiempo. Filosofía de la perspectiva." *Revista de Occidente*, 5 (1923): 201-217.

————. *Ensayos sobre el progreso*. Madrid: Imprenta de G. Sáez, 1932; Madrid: Dorcas, 1980.

————. *Fundamentos de filosofía e historia de los sistemas filosóficos*. Madrid: Espasa Calpe, 1947.

————. *La estética de Kant*. Madrid: Victoriano Suárez, 1912.

————. *La filosofía de Henri Bergson*. Madrid: Residencia de Estudiantes, 1917; Madrid: Espasa-Calpe, 1972.

————. *La filosofía de Kant: Una introducción a la filosofía*. Madrid: Espasa-Calpe, 1917.

————. "Las dos fuentes de la moral y la religión." *Revista de Occidente*, 111 (1932): 270-284.

————. "Sobre la intuición bergsoniana." *Revista General*, 20 (1918): 19-22.

Gay Armenteros, Juan C. *La España del siglo XX*. Madrid: Edi, 1986.

Gullón, Ricardo. "The Generation of 1936." Trans. Francis L. Trice. In *Spanish Writers of 1936 (Crisis and Commitment in the Poetry of the Thirties and Forties): An Anthology of Literary Studies and Essays*, 7-16. Edited by Jaime Ferran and Daniel P. Testa. London: Tamesis, 1973.

Guy, Alain. "Der spanisch Krausismus als religiöse Grundhaltung." *Krause-Tagung* (Hofgeismer, Evangelische Akademie, 27-29 November). Reprinted as "Le krausisme espagnol, comme attitude religieuse." *Les Études Philosophiques* (April 1983): 209-216.

————. *Historia de la filosofía española*. Barcelona: Anthropos, 1985.

————. "La théorie de la religation selon Xavier Zubiri." *Bulletin Hispanique*, 3-4 (1964): 391-395.

————. *Les philosophes espagnols d'hier et d'aujourd'hui*. Toulouse: Privat, 1956.

————. *Los filósofos españoles de ayer y de hoy*. Buenos Aires: Losada, 1966.

————. "Manuel García Morente ou le bergsonisme chrétien." *Bulletin de la Société des Sciences, Lettres et Arts*, 136 (1980): 265-278.

————. "X. Zubiri. Notre attitude à l'égard du passé." In *Le temps et la mort dans la philosophie espagnole contemporaine*, 29-48. Edited by A. Guy and A. Serves. Paris and Toulouse: Privat, 1968.

Hispanic Foundation of the Library of Congress. *La obra impresa de los intelectuales españoles en América (1936-1945)*. Palo Alto, California: Stanford University Press, 1950.

Höllhuber, I. *Geschichte der Philosophie im spanischen Kulturbereich*. Munich: Reihnard, 1967.

Izquierdo Ortega, Julio. "Pensadores españoles fuera de España." *Cuadernos Americanos* (January-February 1965).

López-Morillas, Juan. *El Krausismo español, perfil de una aventura intelectual*. Mexico: Fondo de Cultura Económica, 1956.

————. *The Krausist Movement and Ideological Change in Spain*. Trans. Frances M. López-Morillas. Cambridge, England: Cambridge University Press, 1981.

López Quintás, Alfonso. *Filosofía española contemporánea*. Madrid: Biblioteca de Autores Cristianos, 1970.

Marías, Julián. *Filosofía española actual: Unamuno, Ortega, Morente, Zubiri*. 3rd ed. Madrid: Espasa-Calpe, 1956.

————. *La Escuela de Madrid: Estudios de filosofía española*. Buenos Aires: Emecé, 1959.

Martín Buezas, Fernando. *La teología de Sanz del Río y el krausismo español*. Madrid: Editorial Gredos, 1977.

Martínez Gómez, Luis. *Bibliografía filosófica española e hispanoamericana, 1940-1958*. Barcelona: Juan Flors, 1961.

Morón Arroyo, Ciriaco. *El sistema de Ortega*. Madrid: Alcalá, 1968.

Muro Romero, Pedro. *Filosofía, pedagogía e historia en Manuel García Morente*. Madrid: Consejo Superior de Investigaciones Científicas, 1977.

Nicol, Eduardo. *El problema de la filosofía hispánica*. Madrid: Tecnos, 1961.

—————. *Historicismo y existencialismo: La temporalidad del ser y la razón*. Mexico City: Fondo de Cultura Económica, 1950.

Ortega y Gasset, José. *Epistolario*. Madrid: Revista de Occidente, 1974.

—————. *España invertebrada: Bosquejo de algunos pensamientos históricos*. Madrid: Espasa-Calpe, 1921. Reprinted in *Obras completas*, vol. 3 (1983): 35-127.

—————. *Estudios sobre el amor*. Madrid: Espasa-Calpe, 1939.

—————. "Guillermo Dilthey y la idea de la vida." Reprinted in *Obras completas*, vol. 6 (1983): 165-214.

—————. *Invertebrate Spain*. Trans. Mildred Adams. New York: Norton and Company, 1937.

—————. *Kant, 1724-1924: Reflexiones de centenario*. Madrid: Revista de Occidente, 1929. Reprinted as *Kant*. In *Obras completas*, vol. 4 (1947): 25-59.

—————. *La deshumanización del arte e ideas sobre la novela*. Madrid: Revista de Occidente, 1925.

—————. *La rebelión de las masas*. Madrid: Revista de Occidente, 1930.

—————. *Meditaciones del Quijote*. Madrid: Residencia de Estudiantes, 1914.

—————. *Meditations on Quixote*. Trans. Evelyn Rugg and Diego Marín. New York: Norton, 1961.

—————. *Obras completas*. 12 vols. Madrid: Revista de Occidente, 1946-1983.

—————. *Rectificación de la República*. Madrid: Revista de Occidente, 1931. Reprinted in *Obras completas*, vol. 11 (1969): 329-450.

—————. *The Dehumanization of Art*. Trans. W. Trask. Garden City, N.Y.: Doubleday, 1956.

—————. *The Revolt of the Masses*. Trans. Anthony Kerrigan. Notre Dame, Ind.: University Press of Notre Dame, 1985.

París, Carlos. *El rapto de la cultura*. Barcelona: Laia, 1983.

————. "La filosofía española en los últimos cincuenta años." *Cuadernos para el Diálogo* (June 1964).

Pina Prata, Francisco Xavier. *Dialética da raçao vital: Intuiçao originária de José Ortega y Gasset*. Lisbon: Livraria Morais, 1962.

Roig Gironella, Juan. *Balmes, filósofo*. Barcelona: 1949.

Romero, Francisco. *Ortega y Gasset y el problema de la jefatura espiritual*. Buenos Aires: Editorial Losada, 1960.

Savignano, Armando. *Unamuno, Ortega, Zubiri: Tre voci della filosofia del novecento*. Naples: Guida Editori, 1989.

Sciacca, Michele Federico. *La filosofía hoy*. 2nd ed. Barcelona: Miracle, 1955.

Thomas, Hugh. *The Spanish Civil War*. New York: Colophon-Harper, 1963.

Torre, Guillermo de. "The Generation of 1936 . . . for the Second Time." Trans. Daniel P. Testa and Carol Dana. In *Spanish Writers of 1936 (Crisis and Commitment in the Poetry of the Thirties and Forties): An Anthology of Literary Studies and Essays*, 17-21. Edited by Jaime Ferran and Daniel P. Testa. London: Tamesis, 1973.

Walgrave, Jan Hendrik. *La filosofía de Ortega y Gasset*. Trans. Luis G. Daal. Madrid: Revista de Occidente, 1965.

Zubiri, Xavier. *Cinco lecciones de filosofía*. Madrid: Alianza, 1980.

————. *Ensayo de una teoría fenomenológica del juicio*. Madrid: Revista de Archivos, Bibliotecas y Museos, 1923.

————. "En torno al problema de Dios." *Revista de Occidente*, 149 (1935): 129-159. Reprinted in *Naturaleza, historia, Dios*, 5th ed., 361-397. Madrid: Editora Nacional, 1963.

————. *Inteligencia sentiente*. Madrid: Alianza, 1980.

————. *Inteligencia y logos*. Madrid: Alianza, 1982.

————. *Inteligencia y razón*. Madrid: Alianza, 1983.

————. "Le problème de l'objectivité d'après E. Husserl. I. La logique pure." Dissertation, Louvain, 1921.

6. Philosophical Works of Special Significance
in Relation to José Gaos's Thought

Aquinas, Saint Thomas. *The Summa Theologica*. 2 vols. *Great Books of the Western World*, vols. 17-18. Chicago: Encyclopaedia Britannica, 1990.

Aristotle. *The Works of Aristotle Translated into English*. Edited by W. D. Ross. London, England: Oxford University Press, 1954.

Augustine, Saint. *The Confessions*. Trans. R. S. Pine-Coffin. Baltimore: Penguin Books, 1961.

―――. *The City of God*. Trans. Marcus Dods. New York: The Modern Library, 1950.

Balmes, Jaime. *Curso de filosofía elemental*. Madrid: 1847. Paris: Garnier, 1860. 4 vols. Barcelona: Imprenta Barcelonesa, 1909-1911.

―――. *Obras completas*. 8 vols. Madrid: La Editora Católica, 1948-1950.

Bergson, Henri. *Essai sur les données immédiates de la conscience*. Paris: Félix Alcan, 1889. Rpt. in *Oeuvres: Édition du centenaire*. Edited by André Robinet. Paris: Presses Universitaires de France, 1959.

―――. *Time and Free Will: An Essay on the Immediate Data of Consciousness*. Trans. F. L. Pogson. New York: Macmillan, 1910.

Berkeley, George. *Dialogues between Hylas and Philonous*. In *The Works of George Berkeley, Bishop of Cloyne*. Edited by Arthur Aston Luce and Thomas Edmund Jessop. 9 vols. London and New York: T. Nelson, 1948-1957.

―――. *Three Dialogues between Hylas and Philonous*. Edited by Robert Merrihen Adams. Indianapolis: Hackett, 1979.

Descartes, René. *Discours de la Méthode*. Edited by Étienne Gilson. 2d ed., Paris: J. Vrin, 1930.

―――. *Discourse on Method and Meditations on First Philosophy*. Trans. Donald Cress. 3rd ed. Indianapolis: Hackett, 1993.

―――. *Discourse on the Method of Rightly Conducting the Reason*. Trans. Elizabeth S. Haldane and G. R. T. Ross. In *The Philosophical Works of Descartes*, vol. 1. Cambridge, England: Cambridge University Press, 1931.

Dilthey, Wilhelm. *Gesammelte Schriften*. Edited by E. B. Groethuysen. Leipzig: Teubner, 1922. 8th ed., Stuttgart: Göttingen, 1979.

―――. *Gesammelte Schriften*. Edited by H. Johach and F. Rodi. Göttingen: Vandenhoeck und Ruprecht, 1982.

Hegel, Georg Wilhelm Friedrich. *Encyklopädie der philosophischen Wissenschaften im Grundrisse*. 3 vols. Boston: D. Reidel Publishing Co., *circa* 1978.

——. *Encyclopedia of Philosophy*. Trans. Gustav Emil Mueller. New York: Philosophical Library, 1959.

Heidegger, Martin. *Being and Time*. Trans. John Macquarrie and Edward Robinson. New York and Evanston: Harper, 1962.

——. *Sein und Zeit*. Tübingen: Niemeyer, 1993.

——. *Über den Humanismus*. Frankfurt a. M.: V. Klostermann, 1947. Tübingen: Niemeyer, 1993.

——. *Was ist Metaphysik?* Bonn: F. Cohen, 1929.

Husserl, Edmund. *Ideen zu einer reinen Phänomenologie und phänomenologischen Philosophie*. Halle a. d. S.: M. Niemeyer, 1913.

——. *Ideas: General Introduction to Pure Phenomenology*. Trans. W. R. Boyce Gibson. London: Allen and Unwin, 1931.

——. *Zur Phänomenologie des Inneren Zeitbewusstseins*. The Hague: Nijhoff, 1966.

Jaeger, Werner. *Aristoteles: Grundlegung einer Geschichte seiner Entwicklung*. Berlin: Weidmann, 1923.

——. *Aristotle: Fundamentals of the History of His Development*. Trans. Richard Robinson. Oxford: Oxford University Press, 1934. 2nd ed., Oxford: Oxford University Press, 1948.

——. *Studien zur Entstehungsgeschichte der Metaphysik des Aristoteles*. Berlin: Weidmann, 1912.

Jaspers, Karl. *Existenzphilosophie: Drei Verlesungen gehalten am Freien Deutschen Hochstift in Frankfurt a. M., September 1937*. Berlin: W. de Gruyter, 1938. 2nd ed., Berlin and Leipzig: W. de Gruyter and Co., 1956.

——. *Philosophie*. 3 vols. Berlin: J. Springer, 1932.

Kant, Immanuel. *Critique of Pure Reason*. Trans. John Miller Drew Meiklejohn. Edited by Vasilis Politis. London: Everyman, 1993.

——. *Kritik der reinen Vernunft*. Edited by Ingeborg Heidemann. Stuttgart: Reclam, 1985.

Krause, Karl Christian Friedrich. *Das System der Rechtphilosophie. Vorlesungen für Gebildete aus allen Ständen*. Edited by Karl David August Röcher. Leipzig: F. A. Brockhaus, 1874.

———. *Das Urbild der Menschheit*. Dresden: In der Arnoldishchen Buchhandlung, 1811.

———. *Entwurf des Systems der Philosophie*. 1804.

———. *System der Sittenlehre*. Leipzig: C. H. Reclam, 1810.

———. *Vorlesungen über das System der Philosophie*. Göttingen: In Commission der Dieterich'schen Buchhandlung, 1828.

Müller, Aloys. *Einleitung in die Philosophie*. Berlin und Bonn: F. Dümmler, 1925.

Scheler, Max. *Der Formalismus in der Ethik und die materiale Wertethik*. 2 vols. Halle a. d. S.: M. Niemeyer, 1913-1916.

Windelband, Wilhelm. *Lehrbuch der Geschichte der Philosophie*. Tübingen and Leipzig: J. C. B. Mohr, 1892. 14th ed., ed. Heinz Heimsoeth, Tübingen and Leipzig: J. C. B. Mohr, 1948.

———. *A History of Philosophy*. Trans. James H. Tufts. New York: Macmillan, 1893. 2nd ed. rev. and enl., New York: Macmillan, 1901.

7. Other Recommended Philosophical Works

Marramao, Giacomo. *Minima temporalia: Tempo, spazio, esperienza*. Milan: Il Saggiatore, 1990.

Masullo, Aldo. *Filosofia del soggetto e diritto del senso*. Genoa: Marietti, 1990.

———. *Il problema del fondamento e la filosofia italiana del Novecento*. Edited by P. Ciaravolo. Rome: Publicazioni del Centro per la Filosofia Italiana, 1992.

———. *Il tempo e la grazia: Per un'etica della salvezza*. Rome: Donzelli, 1995.

———. "Soggetto 'patico' e fine del trascendentale." *Paradigmi* 6.16 (1988).

———. *Struttura, soggetto, prassi*. Naples: Edizioni Scientifiche Italiane, 1994.

Vattimo, Gianni. *La crisi del soggetto nel pensiero contemporaneo*. Milan: Angeli, 1988.

ABOUT THE AUTHOR

Dr. Pio Colonnello is Professor of Theoretical Philosophy at the University of Naples, Italy. His published books include *Heidegger interprete di Kant* (1981), *Croce e i vociani* (1984), *Tempo e necessitá: Ricerche su Kant, Husserl, e Heidegger* (1987), and *La questione della colpa tra filosofia dell'esistenza ed ermeneutica* (1995). He has also published articles in various professional journals, including *Criterio, Sapienza, Kant-Studien*, and *Zeitschrift für Philosophische Forschung*. In 1981 and 1988, the Italian government awarded him the *Premio della Cultura della Presidenza del Consiglio dei Ministri d'Italia*. Dr. Colonnello has presented papers at conferences in Europe as well as in Mexico. He is Consulting Editor of *The Journal of Value Inquiry*.

ABOUT THE OTHER CONTRIBUTORS

Dr. Peter Cocozzella, the translator of this book, is Professor of Romance Languages and Literatures at the State University of New York at Binghamton. He has edited volume 1, *Poemas menores*, and volume 2, *Poemas mayores*, of *Obras castellanas* (1991) and *Obras catalanes* (1970), respectively, by Francisco Moner. Among the subjects of his many published essays and talks are Spanish pre-renaissance and twentieth-century Catalan literature. Cocozzella is a member of the Modern Language Association of America and the North American Catalan Society, as well as a Research Associate of the National Resource Center for Translation and Interpretation of the State University of New York at Binghamton.

Dr. Giovanni Gullace, who introduces this text, is Professor Emeritus of Romance Languages and Literatures at the State University of New York at Binghamton. Among his translations of important works from Italian into English are *The Philosophy of Art*, by Giovanni Gentile, and *Benedetto Croce's Poetry and Literature: An Introduction to Its Criticism and History*, by Benedetto Croce. Gullace, the author of many essays and books on French and Italian literature, has been awarded the *Stella della Solidarietà Italiana* by the Italian government and the *Ordre des Palmes Académiques (Chevalier)* by the French government.

Dr. Myra Moss, the Editor of this volume, is Professor of Philosophy at Claremont McKenna College. Moss has served as Associate Editor of *The Journal of Value Inquiry* and as founding Editor of the Italian special series of the Value Inquiry Book Series (VIBS). She is the author of *Benedetto Croce Reconsidered: Truth and Error in Theories of Art, Literature, and History* and the translator of *Benedetto Croce: Essays on Literature and Literary Criticism*.

INDEX OF NAMES

VIBS

The Value Inquiry Book Series is co-sponsored by:

American Maritain Association
American Society for Value Inquiry
Association for Personalist Studies
Association for Process Philosophy of Education
Center for East European Dialogue and Development, Rochester Institute of
Technology
Centre for Cultural Research, Aarhus University
College of Education and Allied Professions, Bowling Green State University
Concerned Philosophers for Peace
Conference of Philosophical Societies
International Academy of Philosophy of the Principality of Liechtenstein
International Society for Universalism
International Society for Value Inquiry
Natural Law Society
Philosophical Society of Finland
Philosophy Seminar, University of Mainz
R.S. Hartman Institute for Formal and Applied Axiology
Society for Iberian and Latin-American Thought
Society for the Philosophic Study of Genocide and the Holocaust
Yves R. Simon Institute.

Titles Published

1.   Noel Balzer, *The Human Being as a Logical Thinker.*

2.   Archie J. Bahm, *Axiology: The Science of Values.*

3.   H. P. P. (Hennie) Lötter, *Justice for an Unjust Society.*

4.   H. G. Callaway, *Context for Meaning and Analysis: A Critical Study in the Philosophy of Language.*

5.   Benjamin S. Llamzon, *A Humane Case for Moral Intuition.*

6.   James R. Watson, *Between Auschwitz and Tradition: Postmodern Reflections on the Task of Thinking.* A volume in **Holocaust and Genocide Studies.**

7.   Robert S. Hartman, *Freedom to Live: The Robert Hartman Story,* edited by Arthur R. Ellis.   A volume in **Hartman Institute Axiology Studies.**

8.   Archie J. Bahm, *Ethics: The Science of Oughtness.*

9.   George David Miller, *An Idiosyncratic Ethics; Or, the Lauramachean Ethics.*

10. Joseph P. DeMarco, *A Coherence Theory in Ethics.*

11. Frank G. Forrest, *Valuemetrics: The Science of Personal and Professional Ethics.* A volume in **Hartman Institute Axiology Studies.**

12. William Gerber, *The Meaning of Life: Insights of the World's Great Thinkers.*

13. Richard T. Hull, Editor, *A Quarter Century of Value Inquiry: Presidential Addresses of the American Society for Value Inquiry.* A volume in **Histories and Addresses of Philosophical Societies.**

14. William Gerber, *Nuggets of Wisdom from Great Jewish Thinkers: From Biblical Times to the Present.*

15. Sidney Axinn, *The Logic of Hope: Extensions of Kant's View of Religion.*

16. Messay Kebede, *Meaning and Development.*

17. Amihud Gilead, *The Platonic Odyssey: A Philosophical-Literary Inquiry into the* Phaedo.

18. Necip Fikri Alican, *Mill's Principle of Utility: A Defense of John Stuart Mill's Notorious Proof.* A volume in **Universal Justice.**

19. Michael H. Mitias, Editor, *Philosophy and Architecture.*

20. Roger T. Simonds, *Rational Individualism: The Perennial Philosophy of Legal Interpretation.* A volume in **Natural Law Studies.**

21. William Pencak, *The Conflict of Law and Justice in the Icelandic Sagas.*

22. Samuel M. Natale and Brian M. Rothschild, Editors, *Values, Work, Education: The Meanings of Work.*

23. N. Georgopoulos and Michael Heim, Editors, *Being Human in the Ultimate: Studies in the Thought of John M. Anderson.*

24. Robert Wesson and Patricia A. Williams, Editors, *Evolution and Human Values.*

25. Wim J. van der Steen, *Facts, Values, and Methodology: A New Approach to Ethics.*

26. Avi Sagi and Daniel Statman, *Religion and Morality.*

27. Albert William Levi, *The High Road of Humanity: The Seven Ethical Ages of Western Man,* edited by Donald Phillip Verene and Molly Black Verene.

28. Samuel M. Natale and Brian M. Rothschild, Editors, *Work Values: Education, Organization, and Religious Concerns.*

29. Laurence F. Bove and Laura Duhan Kaplan, Editors, *From the Eye of the Storm: Regional Conflicts and the Philosophy of Peace.* A volume in **Philosophy of Peace.**

30. Robin Attfield, *Value, Obligation, and Meta-Ethics.*

31. William Gerber, *The Deepest Questions You Can Ask About God: As Answered by the World's Great Thinkers.*

32. Daniel Statman, *Moral Dilemmas.*

33. Rem B. Edwards, Editor, *Formal Axiology and Its Critics.* A volume in **Hartman Institute Axiology Studies.**

34. George David Miller and Conrad P. Pritscher, *On Education and Values: In Praise of Pariahs and Nomads.* A volume in **Philosophy of Education.**

35. Paul S. Penner, *Altruistic Behavior: An Inquiry into Motivation.*

36. Corbin Fowler, *Morality for Moderns.*

37. Giambattista Vico, *The Art of Rhetoric* (*Institutiones Oratoriae,* 1711-1741), from the definitive Latin text and notes, Italian commentary and introduction by Giuliano Crifò, translated and edited by Giorgio A. Pinton and Arthur W. Shippee. A volume in **Values in Italian Philosophy.**

38. W. H. Werkmeister, *Martin Heidegger on the Way,* edited by Richard T. Hull. A volume in **Werkmeister Studies.**

39. Phillip Stambovsky, *Myth and the Limits of Reason.*

40. Samantha Brennan, Tracy Isaacs, and Michael Milde, Editors, *A Question of Values: New Canadian Perspectives in Ethics and Political Philosophy.*

41. Peter A. Redpath, *Cartesian Nightmare: An Introduction to Transcendental Sophistry.* A volume in **Studies in the History of Western Philosophy.**

42. Clark Butler, *History as the Story of Freedom: Philosophy in Intercultural Context,* with Responses by sixteen scholars.

43. Dennis Rohatyn, *Philosophy History Sophistry.*

44. Leon Shaskolsky Sheleff, *Social Cohesion and Legal Coercion: A Critique of Weber, Durkheim, and Marx.*

45.   Alan Soble, Editor, *Sex, Love, and Friendship: Studies of the Society for the Philosophy of Sex and Love, 1977-1992.*   A volume in **Histories and Addresses of Philosophical Societies.**

46.   Peter A. Redpath, *Wisdom's Odyssey: From Philosophy to Transcendental Sophistry.*   A volume in **Studies in the History of Western Philosophy.**

47.   Albert A. Anderson, *Universal Justice: A Dialectical Approach.*   A volume in **Universal Justice.**

48.   Pio Colonnello, *The Philosophy of José Gaos.*   Translated from Italian by Peter Cocozzella.   Edited by Myra Moss.   Introduction by Giovanni Gullace.   A volume in **Values in Italian Philosophy.**